Trout Hunting

Trout Hunting

Frank Woolner

Winchester Press

Copyright © 1977 by Frank Woolner. All rights reserved.
Published by Winchester Press
205 East 42nd Street, New York, N.Y. 10017

Printed in the United States of America

WINCHESTER is a Trademark of Olin Corporation used by
Winchester Press, Inc., under authority and control of the
Trademark Proprietor.

Library of Congress Cataloging in Publication Data

Woolner, Frank, 1916–
  Trout hunting.
  Includes index.
  1. Trout fishing. I. Title.
SH687.W67   799.1'7'55   76-52733
ISBN 0-87691-196-3

Contents

Preface

The author of any work on angling, and especially on trout fishing, must expect a measure of flak when he is maverick enough to declare that each of the various disciplines are arts in themselves, each worthy of high respect and each an essential course in the education of an all-round angler.

In this book I have attempted to outline trout-fishing techniques from basic live-bait presentation on up through the various arts, not as an "expert" (for the word is chillingly semantic) but as a working angler who has found much joy in each nuance of an enthralling pursuit.

In striving to present a case for *all* trout fishermen—and not for a minority who worship at the shrine of fly casting—there is calculated risk. Some purists will not agree with my premise that worming a small stream, spinning, trolling, and ice fishing can be quite as scientific in execution as the casting of a fly. A few are sure to be unhappy about occasionally acid assessment of betters who have advanced the art. If I have stumbled, I apologize. Truth is, they all stubbed their toes from time to time, and I will stub mine.

Fortunately, I am blessed with understanding colleagues, many of whom privately admit that they share my faint praise for Isaac Walton, my complaint about senseless proliferation of fly pattern, my exhortation to understand all of the techniques prior to adopting one as most satisfying. I owe these good folk a debt of gratitude.

H. G. "Tap" Tapply read the first draft of this manuscript and offered constructive criticism. My brothers, Jack and Dick Woolner, also read—and pulled no punches. Paul Kukonen, a Massachusetts perfectionist and outdoor film producer, was helpful, particularly in the realms of spinning and trolling.

For suggestions and for photos incorporated, I thank these, together with Erwin A. Bauer, Rip Cunningham, Myron Gregory, Lefty Kreh, and Russell Tinsley—all well known as expert anglers. Bob Boillard of Maine and Ken Gebhardt of New York offered information about the latest in ice fishing for trout.

Finally, of course, I am beholden to all of the folk with whom I have fished, the true anglers who are not in print, but who always seem to be there with the right offerings, at the right time.

Most prefaces declare: "I hope the reader enjoys this book as much as I have enjoyed writing it." I won't go that route, because writing is not the easiest of trades. This is the result of on-site research and shoptalk with fine anglers. Hopefully, it is American trout hunting today.

Frank Woolner
Shrewsbury, Massachusetts

Trout
Hunting

1

Charisma-
Men and Trout

No other family of game fishes has so fired the imagination of mankind as the salmonid, which embraces all inland trout, char, and the grand sea-run Atlantic salmon. Human beings, since the first scratchings of history, have expressed an astonishing reverence for these noblest of cold-water warriors.

We read and hear most of four species: the lordly Atlantic salmon, the eastern brook trout, the German brown, and the American rainbow. All are superb, but so are the allied cutthroat and Dolly Varden, the delectable little Rocky Mountain golden, and the power-packed steelhead, which is really a sea-run rainbow that surges up into natal rivers at a time ordained by season.

Some may not agree that trout, char, and salmon should be lumped in one magnificent group, but I see them as a family. I also include landlocks and lakers and the almost extinct eastern aureolus; the little blueback, a refugee from remote ice ages, and the gloriously pugnacious Arctic char, supremely triumphant in the cold lands of muskegs and waters not yet profaned by man.

They are trout! They are the fishes that have moved men's souls for thousands of years, that have inspired a glorious literature and a mystique as astonishing as it is viable.

It is refreshing to note that the aboriginal Indians of our Pacific Northwest venerated the salmon, made it their totem, counted the wheeling seasons by its return to a natal river, and felt that any interruption of a life-giving cycle was chastisement administered by the gods.

While the modern ocean sports fishery sometimes detracts from romance (it is rather difficult to feel any delicate emotion when a silvery fish is swept aboard a boat in a wide-mouthed net, whacked on the head with a miniature baseball bat, and unceremoniously tossed into a community fish box), the excitement of a glorious adventure returns when steelhead forge up the brawling western rivers, and where mesmerized anglers adore the rainbows and brook trout of famous eastern streams. The wonder, the awe, and the reverence is there. It is a thing difficult to describe, because it is deep feeling, an adulation, an emotion no auslander can understand.

In America, most of the golden literature originated in the Catskills, Pennsylvania, New England, and Michigan. This is where it all started, and this is the harvest-home of savants. Every eastern angler breathes his own magic name: Brodhead, Beaverkill, Ausable, Letort, Esopus, Battenkill, Blackwater, Deerfield, Grand Lake Stream, and a host of tiny crystalline ponds or big, bounding wilderness lakes.

Now the glorious adventure moves westward and already there is a generation of trout-fishing specialists fevered by the sparkling rivers of Wyoming and Montana and the clean torrents coursing mountains to reach the Pacific Ocean. Aside from his cowboy hat and his regional accent, a western trout fisherman is blood brother to his eastern cousin. Make no mistake, new legends are being made there and some of the accounts now published, or soon to be published, will be as eagerly cherished as the old eastern classics. Great sport is part of it, yet there is a latter-day phenomenon at work, too.

Grand Lake Stream, Maine. Hal Lyman seeks brown trout and landlocked salmon.

Only in recent years have we seen the emergence of the truly well-traveled angler. Halford was wedded to his English chalk streams. Gordon and Hewitt moved regionally, and La Branche favored the East, but today's best are spanning continents, sampling, observing, and comparing. In our time Joe Brooks was a trailblazer, but now he is followed by a host of almost frightening authorities. For those modern pioneers

Among classic eastern streams, list the Letort near Carlyle, Pennsylvania. (Photo by Lefty Kreh)

with the desire and the funds to explore, a vast new world has opened.

Trout evoke an image and foster a dream; they are precious and beautiful, seldom easy to catch and rarely abundant. Therefore, in fishing, all masters choose a rapier instead of a broadsword, smile scornfully at larcenous guides who suggest such ill manners as foul-hooking or tickling, and release more than they kill. To insult such a magnificent creature by abusing it either physically or by use of an uncouth name would be sacrilege. Charles Waterman has mentioned that trout fishermen tend to use gentle, respectful nouns and adjectives when describing a treasured catch, while black bass anglers are likely to call a trophy "a real hawg!"

True enough, yet I have no quarrel with folk who seek bronzebacks. Perhaps they are right and those of us who worship at the shrine of trout are maudlin sentimentalists—but I don't think so. I've caught a lot of black bass, too, marveled at their pugnacious power, wondered at the fire-opal of their blazing eyes fixed in a flashlight's beam at night—and then released them to be caught again. All game fishes are worthy, and all deserve respect, yet nowhere is this feeling more often imprinted upon an angler's mind than it is during a moment of victory over trout and salmon. It is always triumph stained by a contradictory consciousness of ill-doing; veterans get to that point where release is almost automatic.

Even where a few fish are retained for the table, there is a ritual. Each, upon reaching the end of a trail, is admired as an individual. One is enraptured by the living color and markings of this prize beyond all prizes, by its slick, handsome, functional lines. The master angler breathes deeply and mutters terms of endearment, meanwhile bedding his catch in wet fern or watercress. For a few delicious moments such a man has escaped this clanking, grinding, competitive world and is one with the romantic aborigines who prayed for the souls of the game they harvested.

In a little while I am going to say some harsh things about useless tradition and the outright nonsense occasionally associated with status trout fishing, with the literature, with the instant-experts who profess to know all but have little experience other than that acquired on leased, heavily stocked waters. No soldier should speak of combat unless he has been up under the tracers on a wet, cold, and muddy dawn when the artillery barrage is lifting and a massive tank attack is coming on. One may learn a trade on the drill field, but battle is the payoff. Walton, Venables, Skues, and Halford taught their disciples how to fish, and Gordon, Hewitt, and La Branche added immortal words. They were human, so they had faults, but each and every one was magnificent in his own time.

One thing seems common to all of the prophets: all have been, and are, highly opinionated. This is not so heinous a sin as it appears, since such men are unique. At the very least they think for themselves and reject the silly parroting of useless dogma. Often they are abrasive, a handicap in lifetime but a trait softened by time and study.

There is an unfortunate tendency among classicists to declare that the old masters said it all. They forget that science advances, that the literature is a progressive, living thing, not a dead sea scroll. We have trout-fishing authorities today who so far outstrip the old fellows in expertise and know-how that there is no comparison—and *they'll* go down to defeat, too. A thinking angler must winnow out the truth, he must absorb the best and discard that which is questionable. It is somewhat naive to extoll past greats simply because they pioneered a technique and are adored by bookmen.

Trout literature is extensive; probably no other fish in the world has been so thoroughly studied, described, dissected, sought after, and admired. There are good books and bad books. A few go well, edition after edition, and some deserve to be forgotten quickly because they are sorry mistakes. Allegiance to some ancient opus that teaches nothing and is valuable only to a few zealous students of Elizabethian English is fine if that is a primary mission. However, if an angler cannot understand Isaac Walton, then he should not be required to tilt his head on one side and murmur "How interesting."

Personally, I think Walton's *Compleat Angler* a crashing bore! Skues called him "a miserable old plagiarist," and others have noted that Charles Cotton contributed much of value to the sainted work in its fifth (maybe sixth) most popular edition. It is well documented that Walton repeated almost word for word passages from *The Arte of Angling* published by an unknown author 84 years before Isaac was born.

Walton's many admirers shrug off this outragcous plagiarism by saying that he (and Cotton who later edited and added) turned out a work far superior to anything that had gone before. Undoubtedly true, yet this is literary hedging, a knuckling-under to the concept that thievery should be rewarded.

I find some little passages where Isaac's words, or those of his editors, weave magic, but most of it is dull, pedestrian, and difficult to read and assimilate by anyone other than an incurable romantic enthralled by lost tongues. How many modern anglers care what Venator said to Piscator—or the other way around—unless one is vitally interested in the scragging of stray otters, the catching of carp, the way of a horsehair leader, and the how-to of consorting with a gaggle of milkmaids? I have the awful suspicion that *The Compleat Angler's* stilted prose was contrived and patterned after an earlier blueprint, then tinkered by a herd of stuffy editors down through the centuries. I'll bet Venator really said to Piscator—"For God's sake, Ike, pass that bottle!"

Today's scribblers are not above stealing from one another, but they do so with a measure of subtlety, rearranging each string of words so that nobody cries foul.

The importance of being earnest has been cited as good advice, yet a lot of trout writers have been so earnest as to elicit yawns. A few appear to have fed on manna from Heaven and not mortal fodder. For example, there is the self-appointed historian who practically announces that he is the bearer of Gospel, who still spends much time rewriting the opinions of earlier saints.

Many of the old boys, and a lot of the new ones, were and are so deadly serious about the building of a personal image that joyous reading suffers. These are the fey lads who become so technical and immersed in Latin nomenclature that a reader of average intelligence finds himself nodding. Then there are the name-droppers, no horrendous sin, yet almost rib-tickling when bedroll buddies turn out to be the current kings of Europe, transient dictators, or motion picture celebrities. All have fished with and were bosom buddies of the late Charles Ritz.

Ritz was a talented man. I met him only once and never had the honor of fishing with the little tiger. History and his writings indicate that Grand Charles was one of the world's few actually qualified to bandy the names of the great as close comrades. Ritz dropped names, too, but he punctured the balloons of questionable tacticians. He was, without any doubt, a master angler.

Lee Wulff is quite as straightforward and monolithic; an abrasive, hooded-eyed genius he might well be an untouchable had he not built an expertise on trout and salmon fishing that is overwhelming. You'd better be right if you argue with Lee. If you have a point, then he's eager to listen; if you try to con him, he'll shoot you down in flames.

Although the precious ones are almost bereft of humor, angling is a hilarious business and trout fishing is a mixture of high adventure, sylvan delight, and plain old-fashioned slapstick comedy. Only in very recent years have we seen such brilliant rays of thought-provoking merriment as Ed Zern poking his finger into the ribs of the black-robed preachers, John Voelker (Robert Traver) admitting unadulterated delight laced with humor, and Charles Waterman making fun of his own wind-knots—even though Charley is as good a trout fisherman as ever fell into a pool.

We can still chuckle with Alfred W. Miller (Sparse Grey Hackle) and agree with his observation that trout fishing is always better in print than on a stream. Sparse is scrupulously honest; an admitted romantic, he yet tells it truly and says things that the stuffy brothers must swallow because there is no defense against logic.

Ray Bergman's monumental book, *Trout*, remains recommended reading, generation after generation. Joe Brooks came on strong in fresh and salt water. Only occasionally can the world produce writers who are not afraid to state an opinion and resist status roadblocks. Nobody really loves a pioneer until he is long gone, and then the autumn mist shrouds what really happened.

Theodore Gordon was a little, crotchety whip of a man who was a master angler. He was selfish to the point of disgust—a cranky, self-appointed aristocrat who happened on stage at a time when he was able to overwhelm lesser humans who suffered his ill manners because it seemed camp to do so. That he was an angling genius is never disputed.

Theodore created the Quill Gordon fly, one of America's most classic patterns, but it was a thing worked up to represent any number of emerging mayflies, never a facsimile of any specific insect.

Gordon, introverted and secretive, knew a thing that some of today's rigid match-the-hatch boys are still struggling to solve—he knew that *the exact facsimile is impossible.*

I am fully aware that some grand trout fishermen of today have declared that the Quill Gordon is indeed an exact replica of a specific emerging insect but, if they are right, then it was an accident. The record shows that the great Theodore took a rather sadistic joy in the flummoxing of a multitude. His own writings indicate that he thought this artificial a simulation of a mayfly, period.

It would be easy to provide a quote from Gordon himself, but I think this unnecessary. If you want to believe in fairy tales, it's a pleasant occupation. The man built a fly that

9

Dick Woolner with a rainbow trout from a Cape Cod pond.

would catch trout. He almost certainly laughed at academic anglers who believed that it precisely matched a hatch.

Even the dressing of the Quill Gordon is argued to this day. Traditionally, it is a whisp of upright wood duck flank, a body of light quill (maybe with fine silver tinsel), medium-blue dun hackle fibers for a tail, and the same medium-blue dun cock hackle. However, the hackle of the original was supposed to be "the color of water." But what color is water? It can vary, so we may only assume that the aim was almost no hue at all. The pattern was a type in that it was slightly varied, according to season, by the use of light and dark quill and lighter or darker blue dun hackle. Gordon said as much—when he said anything at all.

Edward Hewitt is another saint of flycasters in America. He was a good man, a wealthy, highly educated feudal baron who managed his own stocked waters. Hewitt's research was thorough and he had both the time and money to do a decent job. His fishing was rarely pursued on well-pounded beats, but on his own enclaves—yet he advanced the art, as did Gordon, and he is rightfully praised as angler and scientist.

Hewitt, through study and photography, showed how an artificial fly appears to a trout as it enters that creature's "window," always assuming that a fish sees much as we do. Many of his theories are corroborated by today's research, and he remains a far greater pioneer than Gordon, if only because he proclaimed his findings to the world while Theodore spoke to a few supposed equals. Edward Hewitt was a teacher, while Gordon was a trout-fishing genius who preferred to remain in the shadows.

George La Branche came on with the dry fly in fast water, and he was right. His teachings apply today, but many forget that the man was a superb flycaster. It wasn't entirely his theories that revolutionized the floating artificial in America, because this gentle master was highly gifted and duffers could not equal his delicate presentation. He was good all the way, in his time, but he was far from omnipotent. Many of La Branche's ideas have been altered, and if he were alive today he would undoubtedly smile and admit pleasant errors.

So would Venables and Skues and Halford. They were just men, cursed by the vanities of humankind and current belief, yet they loved trout fishing above all else and were reasonable enough to see how a technique strange to them might work. Isaac Walton would be astonished and amazed—and joyous. All of the old heroes would be pleased to see that trout still command a position of eminence.

The great angling tale-tellers have always written for love and for the things they believe. There are many timeless classics to consult, and some of them are recent. By all means struggle through Dame Juliana Berners and Isaac Walton.

Steep yourself in the good things that launched a sport—and then come back to the moderns. They're really very good, maybe best of all because, like Walton, they have stolen from the masters and added their own inventions. Some are inspiring writers and more are pedestrian, but none can be dismissed as unworthy of attention. In war, the victors always decide what really happened; in angling, we make saints of those who have preached a creed we want to hear.

It may be impertinent of me to attempt any evaluation of contemporaries, but I will do so, right or wrong. No order of preference, though, because that would be unfair.

In America, Preston Jennings must rank as an immortal, for he was first to initiate a scientific study of stream insects and to seek precise simulation in a fly. Regardless of whether, like me, you feel this an impossible dream, or entirely subscribe to match-the-hatch, there is no doubt that Jennings led the way and contributed much knowledge. Now Ernest Schwiebert, Vincent Marinaro, Charles Fox, and Art Flick have inherited the mantle and have added much to the intelligence of trout fishing.

Never a collector, I still treasure six of Preston Jennings' flies, sent to me by Ken Gebhardt of Peekskill, New York. These masterpieces will never go back to war in the spring spates; they are just too valuable to risk. Jennings, in some angler's Valhalla, may chuckle, since he was a fisherman and, like all of us, he had his moments of madness. Among other things, he insisted that the Royal Coachman was a true facsimile of a living insect and he declared that the Atlantic salmon feeds during its upstream spawning run.

There is Ray Bergman, a guru of American trout fishing if one ever lived. And Joe Brooks, of course. Lee Wulff, Al McClane, Charles Fox, Vincent Marinaro, Art Flick, and Ernest Schwiebert all reach for the stars. Ted Trueblood is masterful, and the late Roderick Haig-Brown cannot be touched in his own field.

Charles F. Waterman is swiftly assuming his place as one of the elite. John Voelker scribbles lofty and lovely literature.

Alfred W. Miller, under the nom de plume of "Sparse Grey Hackle," is incomparable. Read Dana Lamb, Howard T. Waldon II, and Charles Ritz. Nick Lyons is a new one who writes like an angel.

There are so many excellent trout writers. Larry Koller comes on straight from the shoulder with unforgettable stuff. Jim Bashline is our foremost authority on night fishing, and he isn't blinded by moonlight either. Joe Bates meticulously examines flies created to take trout and salmon. Spend a quiet, luxurious evening with Burton L. Spiller, recalled as the poet laureate of grouse hunting, and a trout fisherman admittedly democratic in taste. I am going to neglect a lot of them, because the list is long. Literature is the keystone of classic trout fishing. Read, and enjoy.

The appeal is, of course, both the fish and the environment in which it prospers. Roderick Haig-Brown, who wrote so entrancingly about his western steelhead, dwelled upon the allure of a river, its changing moods, a psychological balm for the souls of men seeking a return to tranquillity. The late Arnold Gingrich, endlessly searching for a particular passage from Walton, offered as one of the grandest lines ever written a bit of business that concludes: "then we sit on cowslip banks, hear the birds sing, and possess ourselves in as much quietness as these silver streams, which we now see glide so quietly by us."

Never a very keen admirer of Isaac, I agree with Arnold Gingrich that much of the magic is cowslips and bird song and silvery streams. I can translate that into fresh green meadow grass and redwinged blackbirds teetering on slim willows, a cold flood and a return to a paradise dimly recalled or hoped for. Every trout or salmon is a mute promise that we still have time, that the wilderness has yet to be conquered. Part of it is associated with the beauty of the fish itself and its delectable flesh on the table.

There is a charisma here that spans our world, a love affair that surmounts the absurdities of discrimination based on wealth, race, creed, and color. It is a mutual affection for the

Joseph D. Bates, Jr., with a 22-pound Atlantic salmon from the River Langá in Iceland. Gillie, left, is Davis Oskarson.

salmonids, all of which fall so easily into the same nice niche. They are living jewels, as entrancing to the farm boy coaxing native squaretails with a coarse line and a worm-baited hook as to the educated adventurer who travels this earth over to seek great fishes.

Trout remain. Nobody bad-mouths them, and he who does will be unpopular. He'll also be wrong, because no other fish on earth has so thoroughly captured the heart of humankind.

2

Pilgrim's Progress

Love affairs, viewed from the sanctuary of middle age and bittersweet memory, are almost impossible to document, because human emotion is a mercurial thing. It is different with trout. Trout are absolutely unique in that a man's initial involvement seldom becomes a wry memory dismissed as the folly of youth. It is simply love at first sight, perpetuated and strengthened through a lifetime. One's affection for this lovely creature steadily increases as the years slide by.

My father was not an ardent trout fisherman, so I inherited no priceless literature, tackle, techniques, and burning desire— yet it all happened quite naturally. In the wonderful days of my youth, back in the mid-twenties, all country boys went fishing. Generally we sought the ubiquitous yellow perch of our Massachusetts ponds, the bluegills, horned pout, and chain pickerel that were so plentiful then, and now. Our open-water season started immediately after ice-out, and transportation was either shank's mare or bicycle. In the winter we fished through the ice, chopping our holes with axes, and there were always a few magical days in mid-December when the covering was so thin and transparent that we could stun a loafing

15

pickerel with the concussion of an axe head hammered into the dark mirror. We were all adventurers, ten-year-old disciples of Kit Carson. We ranged like Vikings in our limited territory, and how we escaped drowning is a testimonial to miracles.

In the beginning, where open water was concerned, my buddies and I used birch "poles," carefully selected and then cut to ideal proportions with Barlow jackknives. Line was green linen twist, wound around the tip, and hooks were the simple Japanned models still readily available in those awful "complete professional outfits, including tackle box," for $4.98. Floats were bottle corks, wheedled or simply borrowed from the family medicine closet, and angleworms served as bait.

I simply can't recall anybody ever fishing with the traditional bent pin and sewing thread. It may have happened, but it was before my time. As a matter of fact, in recent years—plagued by a desire to see if it really worked—I fashioned some hooks from common pins and bent a hank of light cotton thread to a sapling. It worked, with a little care, so long as the sapling was no more than a switch.

We weren't entirely naive in that time: all of us had Sears Roebuck or Montgomery Ward catalogs. We managed to acquire second-hand copies of *Field & Stream* and the old *Hunting & Fishing*, which then sold for a nickel. Each winter season saw hectic scanning of the ads and requests for brochures. I can still recall the thrill in reading literature sent by Hildebrandt Spinners, Creek Chub, and Heddon. Those fine old firms invested in the future by providing free catalogs for youngsters who were destined to grow up and become anglers with money to spend.

Not that we lacked money! By February we'd pored over the latest Sears enticement and sent our carefully hoarded coppers for such things as green twisted linen and enameled silk fly lines, for the latest "luminous revolving spoons," spears, minnow traps, and perhaps even a telescoping steel

On Maine's Grand Lake Stream Arnold Laine "bows" to a jumping landlock, while Frank Woolner offers encouragement.

rod. That was the primary weapon with which I initiated my trout-fishing career.

The spears, of course, were for suckers. We started each season with those swarming spawners as they came coursing up the streams. Don't knock it unless you've waded a cold flood in late March or early April, searching out the shadowy monsters in the flickering light of a carbide lantern—and then darting a three-pronged spear with all the derring-do of Queequeg hitting a whale. It was perfectly legal at the time, and a hard, spring-run sucker is delicious table fare. I have eaten many of them and no gourmet meal has ever seemed more delectable.

There was a time when smelt superseded suckers, and then the armament was a dip net in addition to that foul-smelling carbide lantern. Now and then, gloriously criminal, one of us would strike a trout. We always swore that it was a mistake, since we were aware of the law, but the fish tasted pretty good. How else was a kid able to capture a trout?

At that time, and I must have been about ten years old, I recall eavesdropping on a conversation between two really "old" codgers in their twenties. Incredulously, they were discussing the business of catching trout *on flies*! I reported this phenomenal intelligence to a friend but neither of us could quite figure the art of threading a housefly on our oversized Japanned barbs.

Trout remained inaccessible; they seemed to be fish beyond our capabilities—strange, exotic creatures secretly harvested by old guys who were not too fond of kids and who carried many-jointed, multitudinously wrapped split-bamboo fly rods in wooden cases. Evidently one simply did not "go fishing" for trout; the game was a sort of holy rite, reserved for a select company of gentlemen like the local country doctor, a bootlegger who wore a diamond ring as big as a quail's egg, and a couple of ne'er-do-wells who slept with bird dogs—and looked and smelled it.

Johnny Polleski initiated me. He was maybe 19 at the time, the son of an immigrant Lithuanian. His right name was Pucilauskas, but when his father came over from Europe, some arrogant and officious personnel manager in a steel plant couldn't pronounce the tongue twister, so he said, "Your name is Polleski!" The family is still divided, some going under the original, and some the bestowed name.

Johnny was a talented musician and a budding cartoonist. More important, from my viewpoint, he befriended a kid with an insatiable desire to conquer a squaretail trout.

We went first to a meadow stream called Bonny Brook in the township of Grafton, Massachusetts. Bonny Brook was nowhere more than 6 feet in width and often dwindled to a crystal trickle under alders and marsh grass. Its origin was a clear spring under a hill, and there one could always see fingerling trout darting about in air-clear depths.

Nowadays, a visit induces nausea, for so-called "progress" has ensured a revolutionary change. On the enclaves of Bonny Brook Farm—which may have given the stream its name, or maybe the other way around—an industrial complex was located during the thunderous years of World War II. Industry swiftly changed the bright water into a sewer of discharged oils and chemicals. It is now as polluted and defiled as ever a place can be. No trout can live there. Indeed nothing can live there, other than mosquitoes—and they probably have a hard time.

But when Johnny Polleski and I arrived, back in the late twenties, it was three miles of clear, cold, potable water. Squaretails lived there, and only squaretails; at the time, Massachusetts fisheries people had not begun to stock rainbows and browns. A very great percentage of the population was native, as handsomely marked and salmon-fleshed as any aboriginal char of the wilderness. They weren't very big: a 10- or 12-incher was a prize, and the average ran to maybe 7 or 8. At that time we could take fifteen per day, and often did.

It was all worm fishing, and not very sophisticated. Johnny taught me to approach a pool carefully, never letting my shadow fall across it, and he stressed the need for a quiet approach so that no bank vibrations would alarm the spooky fish. These commandments endure, although we have better tackle now and we can do things that were impossible with the old oil-treated silk line and a short gut leader.

I caught my first trout in a deep-gouged pool between an earthen dam and a trolley-car track—the track even then long neglected and retired. The willows grew up on either side and the flood swirled mightily. Brookies held at the tail of the pool, and they were patsies for a worm-baited hook dropped

Circa 1947—Snake Pond, Maine, where squaretails ranged up to 6 pounds.

well above and drifted in. With reasonable stealth you could always take two or three before the remainder of the tribe spooked.

Guided by my benefactor's instructions, I crawled through the lush grass and clover that carpeted that old dam and carefully dropped a worm-baited hook into the tinkling head of the run. Line rattled through glass guides and then paused as my offering reached quiet depths just ahead of the trolley-car embankment. That's where squaretails were placidly finning in a shadow line, feeding on whatever the current provided.

I felt a sudden twitch, and then another. Quite suddenly there was a determined little run, and Johnny yelled—"Hook him!"

Ultralight was then as remote as a space vehicle, and we didn't mess around with "playing a fish" or using a landing net. I heaved mightily, absorbed a moment of delicious, writhing tension, and then my 8-inch trout came sailing out like a missile to arc directly over my head and plummet into the clover.

I pounced on that prize like a fox on a mouse, and Polleski chuckled. You know something? That old boy still chuckles like a lunatic when he recalls all of the trips we made together, a young man and a kid, sharing the immaculate abundance of an unspoiled countryside. Some of the safaris were heroic by today's standards.

It's been a long time since that first trout, and I have been fortunate enough to have fished in fresh and salt water all over this hemisphere—Atlantic salmon in Canada, trophy striped bass in an explosive New England surf, bonefish on Florida's turquoise flats, marlin and bluefin tuna, tarpon, and roosterfish from Canada to the offshore rips of Central America. But none of the supposedly great ones have made so lasting an impression as that first trout.

It was simply the most desirable of fishes: dark, reticulated olive-green above, shading into charcoal and crimson on the flanks above a white belly. There were ruby and golden spots, fins edged with pearl. Although the term was then alien, my perch, bluegills, and pickerel suddenly became "coarse fish." I only knew, as I caressed this grandest of prizes, that no other conquest had ever been so beautifully formed, so soft-hard and slick and functional, so magnificently colored, so absolutely satisfying. At that moment I was hooked as thoroughly as my midget squaretail.

Thereafter, although there were seasonable expeditions into the bailiwicks of perch and bass and pickerel, brook trout usurped a lot of time and became paramount targets. In the beginning, for me, it was all Bonny Brook, and I explored it from that headwater spring to the point where it flowed into Lake Quinsigamond. Gradually, and we all do this, I learned something about pools and how they are formed. I even learned a little about the nature of brook trout, but it was all trial and error. The magnificence of discovery needed no guiding literature. In any event, I had none. Country kids, unless their fathers were avid anglers, were then totally ignorant of the Hewitts, the Gordons, and the Bergmans. In my day there were few library volumes to offer instruction. We went in cold, literally.

The brook was about 3 miles from my home, and I either hoofed it down there or used a bicycle. I had a steel telescoping rod with red glass guides, a cheap single-action reel, a level enameled fly line, and hooks snelled to short gut leaders. Practical willow creels were then available at prices that would cause moderns to drool, and I had one. The creel, I think, is now phasing out, probably due to the fact that a majority of enthusiasts release most of their catch, yet a handsomely fashioned model is something of a collector's item—and expensive.

Our bait never varied—angleworms or nightcrawlers. Worms were spaded up in last year's tomato patch or chicken run. The crawlers provided a sport in themselves because we hunted them at night after a spring shower. People still do this, so never question the flashlight beam moving across a golf course or suburban lawn in the deep night. A fisherman is seeking bait, and enjoying a measure of challenge in doing so.

First, unless you're an abject defeatist, load for bear. This means a decent flashlight and an adequate container. The best, for an incurable romantic, is a large and empty tomato can with a handful of soil for bedding. You may, if you so desire, go to a space-age plastic vessel, but it won't be the same. Some sticklers used to feel that the only gentlemanly container was a Prince Albert tobacco can. Nightcrawlers deserve respect and there is much to be said for tradition.

Man or boy can approach this battleground well swathed in foul-weather gear and rubber boots. Admittedly, protective garb prevents a measure of messiness, but there is something immeasurably exciting in the sweep of a warm rain that wets the crusader from pate to ankle while he challenges his adversary on more or less even terms. A nightcrawler is mighty low on the totem pole of creation, yet it is no easy mark for professors of zoology who spend too much time theorizing instead of acting. A small boy, well indoctrinated by foulmouthed colleagues, is predator supreme: he goes in like a fighter pilot, eyes bulging, finger on the trigger. He's quick and sure. Too bad that, with maturity, we tend to get stuffy.

There are rules to observe. In a real gully washer, nightcrawlers come all the way out and may be plucked at random. If the precipitation is thin, or maybe if the soil is only slightly moistened by a heavy dew, they will be halfway in and halfway out of their burrows.

If you can grab and snatch a nightcrawler in one quick movement, then it is likely to be hauled from its burrow intact. However, the slightest hesitation in yanking will cause that creature to expand its fuselage so that the end result will be a broken squirmer. The trick is to snatch a crawler and dump it into a tomato can before it knows what has happened. Small boys do it well, and those of us who are graying at temple and brain with too much specialized nonsense are defeated.

Some of today's pampered angling brats may shake their heads, but when I was a sprout there were no waders or even hip boots. We slogged through the awakening swamps in tennis shoes, or "sneakers," wincing at every first, frigid inundation—and then accepting it as part of the suffering that one must undergo in order to enter paradise. That it was, and still can be, paradise, I am willing to argue the affirmative. Those of us who forget the feel of mud between our toes and the rush of clean water in a green, gold, and blue wilderness are beyond redemption.

In retrospect, I am sure that the sun was always warm, and there were always redwinged blackbirds teetering, sounding a melodious o-ka-lee. Meadow larks flushed out of lush fields where the first buttercups lifted chalices of pure gold, and black ducks spattered away, harshly protesting invasion of their privacy. First of the legions, there were marsh marigolds or cowslips guarding the skunk cabbages—and I still delight in the scent of an early skunk cabbage crushed in hand. It is the scent and essence of a northern springtime.

At a vernal equinox, progress is rapid. The fresh grasses are sprouting and there are wild blue flags, plus a few yellow ones undoubtedly planted by some pioneer long buried in a rocky hill side cemetery. The early black bees hum around opening flowers and no-see-ums attack in clouds as fine as drifting pepper. Handicaps? I remember the trout!

They were marvelous things of a clean wilderness, fish to stalk as an Indian brave might have approached his prey, to hook and to land, and then to treasure. Every boy harbors a killer instinct, slowly modified by years and the miracle of creation. I found myself bedding those trophies in wet beds of soft grass, fern, and watercress. Later, I marveled at the imprint of fern or grass etched into a squaretail's skin color at the end of a fruitful morning. How delicious they were, both to look at and then to eat golden-brown out of a frying pan anointed with butter.

No modern, sophisticated trout fisherman is more completely enraptured than those of us who essayed the sport with rough tackle. Many of us return, vainly attempting to regain this paradise lost, and we rarely succeed. Almost every one of the great trout writers occasionally scribbles a nostalgic piece about days long lost, but not forgotten. For example, I have never met Ted Trueblood, but I count him a kindred soul because he goes back to the joys of early season small-stream bait fishing in his western mountains. It isn't necessary for me to discuss the matter with Ted, because I just know that he is no instant-expert, that he can handle any tackle thrust into his hand or score with any firearm. He is a true sophisticate who remembers his basics.

24

John Polleski is a lifelong angler, too, and I honor him because he initiated me into a new discipline. Johnny, who was then attending a business school, still found time to go fishing, and he must have been a singularly forgiving youth to pardon the trespasses of an ardent youngster as a companion. In those days, we must have been pretty short of shekels, because we usually walked to our chosen streams even though there were trolley cars available for nickels. At that time we never felt underprivileged, and we undertook journeys that would appall moderns. One in particular remains in memory.

We'd planned to fish a stream two townships away, at least 15 miles from home base. That morning it rained—in fact, the heavens opened floodgates—yet we hiked those 15 miles to our destination. No foul-weather gear, and no boots! Johnny and I were soaking wet in ten minutes, but it was a warm downpour and a great adventure. Angleworms were sluiced across the blacktop, and we gathered some of them to augment our supply as we trudged along. There were automobiles, but nobody offered to pick us up, and we never lifted a thumb.

The stream was predictably high and roiled by the flood, but trout were on a feeding spree. They were all squaretails at the time, and we lined our creels with good limits. And then we walked home through the pouring rain.

Lifelong anglers willingly admit that they fell in love with trout at an early age, say about four years before they were smitten by girls. It's a feeling that remains for as long as they live. They may go through some dangerous times, because a lot of mothers and wives can't understand the siren song of a tumbling stream. Although, in courting, they have admired outdoor life and angling, once spliced the average wife cannot cope with a husband who returns late, wet and bedraggled with a stubble of whiskers and a couple of little squaretails in a dripping creel. There is absolutely no way to explain the magic of a green and gold paradise, the ducks thundering out, the little, dipping cadence of grasses over a pool, or even a hatch that developed late and had to be attended, because it might never happen again.

Anxious parents should experience no qualms over youngsters who are addicted to tweaking fishes out of stream or pond. Such a kid has little time for such youthful aberrations as stealing automobiles, destroying private property for the pure joy of vandalism, and otherwise pestering a patient establishment. Not only that, but unless they are silly enough to fall into a deep pool and get drowned, angling is a pretty safe pastime, actually far less perilous than many team sports.

Today's kids are healthier and smarter than we were. If there is fault it lies in parents who expect their offspring to fly a fighter before they master a trainer. It is far better to go in with the basics and progress step by step. There is really nothing wrong with a light cane pole or with a simple, telescoping steel rod armed with an easily handled reel and a line that will do the job without professional expertise. Such equipment is still readily available, but is too often deemed "not good enough for our son." As a result, a large percentage of potentially grand anglers are turned off at the very beginning.

Introduce youngsters to the sport with crude gear. Let them master the trainers as they move up. Progress is always rapid, and a youngster who is hooked on trout will soon clamor for more sophisticated gear. The step-by-step procedure ensures skill, or at least a working arrangement with each of the disciplines. The man who pushes his youngster into an advanced technique may well guarantee that kid's lifetime hatred of angling. It isn't sport if it isn't fun.

I still remember the rod that was my passport to fly-fishing. Before the telescoping steel rod had been scorned, some distant relative gave me a split-bamboo beauty, an ancient Hardy tastefully adorned with many wrappings. Gradually it fell apart—the result of youthful abuse—but I still have the German silver ferrules and reel seat. Like the gunner who sold an heirloom Parker double-gun for a pittance, or let it rust into oblivion, I could almost weep about a rod that would be a collector's item today.

With that rod I used artificials for the first time and found that they could be effective. The lines were still oil-treated silk, prone to get sticky when ill-treated, and there were gut leaders that had to be thoroughly soaked prior to any effective use. Reels haven't changed all that much, although a then cheap Meiselbach I owned is now eyed with envy by graying colleagues. The standby single-action winch then, as now, was Pflueger's remarkable Medalist. No reel has ever returned so much value for so little money.

At that time Gordon, Hewitt, and La Branche had alerted the fly-fishing world to new departures and Halford had loftily proclaimed his techniques as the last word. Ray Bergman was writing stirring articles, but had yet to publish his monumental *Trout*. There were other authorities and all of them seemed strangely remote, like gods on Olympus. They didn't speak our language or, better stated, we weren't attuned to receive.

The flies were a romance in themselves and had a medley of famous names: Jock Scott, Royal Coachman, Silver Doctor, Black Gnat, Parmachene Belle. In the beginning, each was carefully snelled on a short length of heavy gut with a perfection loop knot that created bubbles when bent to the end of a leader or arranged as a dropper. Dry flies were still beyond us, and we used the wet patterns because most of the popular literature screamed that this was the way to catch trout.

We didn't take many on flies, since we didn't know how to use them. Each conquest was a triumph in itself, proof that we had graduated and become master anglers. Actually, I think a majority of us were mesmerized (and remain so) by the beauty and promise of intricate patterns. There was, and still is, a secret and savage joy in admiring the fly tyer's intricate marriage of exotic feathers, fur, tinsel, and craft. It is almost as good to see these creations in a folded, sheepskin-lined packet as to cast them upon the waters.

Fly-fishing apprentices—and I am included—often carried a little can of angleworms, just in case. It was good to fight chivalrously, but ego deflating to return with empty creels. Long years ago, after I had graduated from the era of the telescopic rod but was still intrigued by worming a tiny meadow stream best described as a woodcock run, I met an angler who always said that his best catches were made on a Black Gnat. Curiously, when encountered on a stream, he always had a worm-baited hook on his line.

One day when the recurrent story of the Black Gnat's efficiency was being related to a group of wide-mouthed colleagues, I probably made a lifelong enemy by inquiring: "Was that Black Gnat male or female?"

He halted in mid-sentence and peered at me as though I had sprouted green antennae. "For Cri-sakes," he said, "it's just a little black fly!"

I figured, privately, that he was still carrying a can of angleworms in his back pocket.

It took me a lot of years to progress beyond live bait to the thrill of dry flies and wet flies and nymphs. There were years of deep and shallow trolling, plus experimentation with the new art of spinning. I don't regret a day of it because it was the learning of a trade, an art, and a science. I do not hold one method superior to another; they are all tremendously complicated and effective. It is wise to sample all methods prior to arguing the virtues of one. Who says that fly-fishing is the only way to catch a trout? Who says that bait-fishing is somehow degrading, and that trolling or spinning is below the ethics of a sportsman? Come on, friends, bigotry is both unpopular and stupid.

Prior to World War II my world was ordered, if somewhat difficult. We struggled through a great depression, yet there was an all-pervading optimism in the future of America. By the mid-thirties I'd progressed to fly-casting as a favored method during the trout-fishing season. There were ruffed grouse in October, deer in November, ice fishing, figure skating, and hockey after winter clamped down. I was then racing cycles all over the country, winning a few tin cups and getting clobbered on roads and tracks. A well-meaning impresario wanted me to turn pro and repair to the Velodromo Milano in Italy, but war seemed imminent.

On December 7, 1941, I spent an afternoon shooting skeet. Half across our world the shooting was far removed from a Sunday's sport—and that was truly an end of an era. For me, the familiar "Greetings" arrived within weeks. Induction was both expected and welcome. I chose tanks and spent almost four years with the Third Armored Division of the United States First Army, progressing from stateside training to England, thence to a Normandy beach-head and five major campaigns before we halted on Germany's River Elbe. For six months after the Reich's collapse, I remained in Germany to write *Spearhead in the West*, the narrative history of my division in action.

When I was mustered out of Germany in a blizzard on the last day of November in 1945, I was a far different man. Nothing was as it had been; even hunting and fishing had changed. Now there were tubular fiberglass rods and synthetic lines, nylon leaders that required no soaking but wouldn't sink as the old silkworm had. It was an exciting period, marred only by the sobering realization that America had changed and had become a world power, with all of the problems and responsibilities associated with that cataclysmic revolution.

Among other things, there was a rush to produce at the expense of a living environment. Bonny Brook was a microcosm, yet a portent: it lay stinking and dead under the discharged wastes of industry. One had to go farther and farther afield to visit clean waters, and the devouring economy raced toward limbo. Pollution ranged from the haphazard application of deadly insecticides to a callous destruction of all natural resources in the name of progress.

True, scientific anglers had arrived; we enjoyed the tools and the literature, plus rapid transportation to our favorite fishing sites. Spinning tackle began to challenge basic plug and fly, primarily because it was the "easy way," a cure-all for the

The author, a bicycle racer in youth, used his track machine to combine road training and trout fishing.

incompetent. Actually, it was neither of these things, but the myth is perpetuated to this day. Men are always intrigued by something for nothing, and there is a universal delusion that one may succeed without education. The better practitioners knew better then, and now. For that reason we currently see a burgeoning interest in all of the disciplines, with no one of them acknowledged all-purpose. Purists, whatever the technique, are narrow-minded zealots, akin to the clerics of dark ages who argued the number of angels who could dance on the head of a pin.

Americans have now far outstripped Europeans and the rest of the world in sportfishing tackle and tactics. We have the finest gear ever manufactured on earth and our authorities are flexible and innovative. If they haggle and disagree, that is good; in so doing, these craftsmen propose new concepts based on experience.

Economics aside, we go fishing primarily for the joy of melting into a natural fluvial landscape and reverting back to a dimly recalled rapport with the wilderness. It is regenerating to leave the clattering cities behind and escape to a place where the birds are singing, flowers are blooming, and a man is just another beneficent savage among savages. Our space-age tackle is window dressing.

The joy endures, and the trout is forever held in some sacred, secret niche of the mind. A trout is, admittedly, just a fish, a worthy adversary on light tackle and a challenge to any angler. But it is also one of America's sacred treasures, a companion to the beaver, the white-tailed deer, the ruffed grouse, and the long-lost buffalo herds. In short, it is a symbol of the grand wilderness we seek to preserve forever. It is tranquillity in a hurry-hurry world. And no matter how encountered, that first magnificent prize will always remain in memory, a gift of the gods, a fish beyond mortal description.

Now it is possible to board a jet and fly to some edge-of-the-world location to take fish that crowd the world's all-tackle record mark. I'm a pretty fair fisherman myself. I have a nodding acquaintance with all of the disciplines and I have caught a lot of grand warriors in fresh and salt waters across the face of the earth. But there is one thing I can never do again, and that is recapture the thrill of first encounter and first love.

31

How delightful and soul-satisfying it would be to go back and hoist one's first 8-inch brookie, gleaming and hard and beautiful, over a moldering earthen dam into a field of clover where the bees are humming and the world is one fresh, grand symphony of warm spring sunlight. *That* would be paradise regained.

3

Experts and Anglers

What, really, is a trout-fishing expert? Is he always the popular writer regularly published? Writers can be craftsmen with rod and line, but it doesn't follow that they are always great anglers. A few meet every requirement and these men are properly acclaimed. But beware of the man who is narrow, who latches on to one method and either scorns or ignores all others; he hasn't learned the trade, he's a taster.

It is unfortunately true that there are hosts of self-appointed experts, plus smaller gaggles of celebrities adored by the public and therefore awarded reverence ill-deserved. Motion-picture actors and television personalities, big-league athletes, famous generals, and politicians need only be photographed, rod in hand, to qualify as authorities. Many seek no adulation as anglers and shrug it off as necessary public-relations hoopla. Some are exceptionally good.

Ted Williams, for example, may be one of the finest all-round anglers in the world. Still a splendid physical specimen, but no longer a "splinter," this baseball immortal is almost as proficient with a fishing rod as a baseball bat. He's done it all,

*Ex-baseball great Ted Williams fishing a Massachusetts club
pond in the mid-40s.*

fresh water and salt, all over the world. Undoubtedly Ted can be topped in a specific technique, but only by the best.

Years ago, when Ted Williams was a Boston Red Sox superstar, before he donated the best years of his life to the Marine Corps and the cramped cockpit of a Vought-Corsair, I watched him fish for trout. He was good then, much better than average, and he had yet to travel widely.

Now, when I meet this man whom I consider the greatest hitter in baseball history, a cinch to have outblasted both Babe Ruth and Hank Aaron had not a couple of wars interfered, we don't discuss Doubleday's folly. We talk about fishing and hunting.

Ted used to spar with sportswriters, but some of them gave him bad marks. He is gung ho and impulsive, sometimes abrasive, but he understands fishing and can handle any of the tackle.

Vern "Gadabout" Gaddis was a superb angler long before he became a national TV personality with his down-to-earth fishing shows. Gaddis related to the masses because he found joy in each technique and bad-mouthed none. Vern is one of the few impresarios who can hold one's interest even when televising a water-haul where no fish are caught. Elation in the hooking and releasing of midget trophies, in addition to a few heavyweights, makes him warmly human.

Curt Gowdy, crack TV sports announcer and long-time anchorman of "The American Sportsman" series, bows to few in the expertise of fly-fishing for trout. Gowdy, like all showmen, dotes on hero worship, but don't bother him with requests for autographs when he is stalking a wary brown or rainbow.

I do not know nor have I ever met Bing Crosby, yet Curt tells me that the famed crooner is hard to top with a fly rod. Gowdy also awards laurels to golfers Jack Nicklaus and Sam Snead. Great athletes who get hooked on fishing usually prosper; they are superb physical specimens to begin with, their reflexes are honed, they are people who always ride to win and hate second place. All listen to reputable guides, skippers, and instructors, and they dedicate themselves to mastering the science of angling.

Shake hands, some time, with ex-heavyweight boxing champion Jack Sharkey. His huge right fist feels like a broken bag of bones, but Sharkey throws a delicate fly line and it wouldn't be wise to wager with him on a trout stream. Jack is a passionate flycaster and, although aging, his reflexes remain far faster than those of the average man. One night, in the smoky press room of a metropolitan sportsmen's show, I witnessed an enlightening exhibition.

Arthur Sullivan, the popular outdoor editor of Boston's *Herald-American*, a true leprechaun of the daily press and an old friend of Sharkey's, decided to clown around. "You're a has-been," he roared at Jack and, assuming a boxing stance, "for two bits I'd belt you right on the whiskers!"

Sharkey, his pale, pouched eyes twinkling, turned slowly away, as though he couldn't be bothered. Then suddenly the left jab came out of nowhere, faster than any snake could strike. Carefully, the old champ missed by a hair and, as Sully involuntarily dropped his guard and ducked, the right cross whistled in, again carefully missing by scant inches!

It was an impressive performance. The champ is old and beat up, but he's still quick. No wonder Jack Dempsey held him one of the toughest men he ever faced in a squared circle.

There is a sort of reverse-snob syndrome going where celebrities are concerned; perhaps it is human nature to wonder about the qualifications of big names in a field other than that in which they initially excelled. However, any athlete who truly embraces angling has the tools. So do ex-fighter pilots, who have instant perception. Such men zero-in quickly; their reflexes are superior and their thought processes ballistic and rapid.

Only a dolt ignores the authorities, yet a lot of today's pooh-bahs offer a minimum of practical innovation, plus a

An Alaskan steelhead spatters into the air. (Photo by Erwin A. Bauer)

maximum of outmoded dogma. In angling, it is all fly casting! In fact, much of our current literature is a regurgitation of things said long ago by Walton, Halford, Skues, Gordon, Hewitt, and Jennings. Worse, there are volumes on techniques that every country flycaster has recognized for a hundred years, new departures of flies actually developed before the authors were spawned, inventions long since invented, theories

37

argued by Isaac Walton and his friends over mugs of ale. And every romantic word of it is dedicated to the spoofing of trout with a fly.

Nobody seems to recognize the fact that other techniques are both artistic and deadly, or that about 90 percent of modern trout hunters fish with natural baits, spinning lures, or a hodgepodge of trolled offerings. The science of trout fishing in most of our literature thus boils down to a single discipline —admittedly entrancing, but still the choice of a minority. I protest. It is my feeling that a master should know all of the methods, from such methods as tickling and spearing on up through the use of natural baits in tiny trickles to big floods, through bottom-bouncing and trolling and spinning to ice fishing. If you prefer to use nothing other than a fly, that is your business, but you ought to have a nodding acquaintance with the whole system.

As an upland hunter I no longer shoot grouse on the ground, yet it would be a lie to say I *never* did in youth. Similarly, I have tickled trout, speared them, killed them with hand grenades—also long ago and recalled with no pride. I never used, or saw used, dynamite. That it works is documented, but I want no part of it. When you play with high explosives, a minor mistake is disastrous, and the same thing applies to homemade electronic shocking devices dreamed up out of old crank-operated telephones. All are illegal, dangerous, and no fun at all—unless you get a thrill out of flummoxing harried game wardens and playing Russian roulette.

A man may also shoot a fish with a gun. It is forbidden in most areas, yet there is more sport in the method because one aims at a specific target. Almost always concussion is the killer, so you shoot a few feet *ahead* of the wake of a fish in shallow water. A shotgun is better than a rifle, but either will do. It is a lousy way to fish and I mention it only because it is done. I experimented in my salad days, but will never do it again unless survival depends on it.

Experts and Anglers

Tickling is another grass-roots art, not very sporting—but note that Edward Hewitt admitted to the practice. Where trout are holding under cut banks, stones, or other cover, anyone who knows the art may dip an arm to the shoulder, "tickle" the resting fish's belly with a cautious hand, and finally grasp it. Lord knows why they accept this indignity, but they do.

Spearing is easy in the cold spates of spring, again usually illegal and the bailiwick of lawbreakers. Foul-hooking, not so often attempted with spooky trout, but on Atlantic salmon lying almost dormant in a holding place, is rampant. A single treble hook, perhaps weighted, is positioned and driven into the fish's flesh. Some renegade guides recommend the process when salmon won't take flies, and some charlatans listen to them. Such folk also buy jacklighted ten-point bucks and bears caught in traps.

Outdoor writers record history, detail know-how and weave romance, but there are legions of magnificent anglers who are inarticulate or never bother to record their thoughts. Those of us in the media too often steal their expertise and project it as our own. If we are honest, we also experiment and sometimes come up with a hopeful breakthrough. No scribbler does it all by himself, and the truly great ones credit their teachers.

Of course, a well-traveled outdoor writer has the edge, if only because his business will take him to great grounds and afford the opportunity to train under fine guides and skilled colleagues. Citizens who make their living in other fields seldom enjoy so thorough an apprenticeship, except for the men of wealth who travel and settle for nothing but the best. Some of them are masters, and others are duffers who count success more important than either sportsmanship or skill.

Some of the world's greatest angling literature has been produced by gentlemen of independent means who focused all of their individual wealth, intelligence, and muscle on solving the mysteries of angling. Very often the true aristocrat is a tough and capable campaigner; he won't be dead wood when the wilderness threatens, and he won't ask others to carry his pack. Remember Teddy Roosevelt in hunting and Ed Hewitt in angling, both born with the proverbial silver spoon in their mouths. They asked no favors.

Sure, some wealthy sports go status and stuffy, insisting on private, well-stocked club streams and ponds, or flying far into the wilderness where trophy trout not only swarm but are eager to attack anything that moves. These lads don't have to be particularly skillful. Many of them *are*, yet many would do a lot of fretful cussing if they had to compete with the peons on heavily pounded, open-to-the-public waters. There, the recognized expert must also be an angler. His victories in the outback, his books and his fame are certainly not taken into account by a wary Catskill brown trout, spooky as a mouse in a cage full of cats.

One very important thing is lost to the holier-than-thou angler: he loses the absolute delight of going into battle as an equal; he can't associate with the folk whose grammar is atrocious, but whose technique on a stream cannot be faulted. The Babbitts scorn anything other than that currently considered camp, and so they lose much magic. Pity them.

Traditionally, to the amusement of all, a barefoot boy with a birch pole and a tomato can full of worms always outfishes the pot-bellied specialist uniformed and bountifully outfitted with the best and most expensive tackle available. This is a tenderly nourished myth worth perpetuating. You won't find many precocious kids who have discovered the keys to a kingdom, yet local adult angler-experts are never very hard to discover.

Such a man may never have visited the exotic grounds and his education may have terminated far short of Groton and Harvard. Maybe he's a barber or a bricklayer in a small town, but he's also the most successful trout fisherman in residence. Effortlessly, he casts a fly well beyond your best grunt-and-

40

Hal Lyman, publisher of Salt Water Sportsman, *lands a small landlocked salmon.*

groan heave, and he does it with tackle that Orvis or Fen-wick might scorn. He knows where the fish live and what they'll take. He's an on-site specialist.

True, the local ace may know a single discipline, or maybe several, all geared to his own stamping ground and all proved by trial and error. He will never write a book or contribute to the magazines. Indeed his literary skill is likely to be exhibited only in the form of a hardly decipherable scrawl to a city friend: "The ice went out yistidday. Get here soon and we will see if them big trout is interested in flies."

Sophisticated guides are quite another thing, and I am not going to sing any paean of praise for guides as a class. The majority are outright opportunists, farm boys or lumberjacks making a quick buck before the potatoes need hoeing or the paper company calls for swampers. A friend of mine once had a guide who lost a mitten on the first day of a deer hunt. For the rest of the week they hunted for a mitten, not for deer.

Nonetheless, there are guides whose skill and intelligence raise the eyebrows of erudite and practical sports. These are gentle, brawny, slow-talking characters who spend a busman's holiday stalking game fishes. They are founts of information, just as eager to absorb instruction as to offer it. They know the conformation of every pool and can just about count down to a strike if your lure or fly is properly cast and worked. These men are both experts and anglers within the narrow confines of home territory.

Residence in the backcountry means little. Almost every small town in the boondocks boasts a few frighteningly efficient practitioners, plus a legion of hacks who will never scale the heights because they subscribe to the idea that "what was good enough for dad is good enough for me." Some, exposed to the literature, or keen enough to see that the sports they guide are highly successful with new techniques, go on to greatness. A healthy majority sticks to handlining, worming, very elementary trolling, and such native nasties as spring spearing and summer tickling. They are inept and, although the finest folk in our world, often express a mixture of astonishment and anger at the sight of a craftsman releasing trout after trout.

Charley Whitney and I used to go up to Sourdnahunk Lake, on the border of Maine's Baxter State Park, every year, not just to fish Sourdnahunk, but to visit it on an itinerary that included many lakes, ponds, and streams during a spring sabbatical. We used nothing but flies and, during our three- or four-day residence, would keep only enough for breakfast. The rest were tenderly released, and we found this astonishing to some natives.

One of the quirks of Sourdnahunk, and certainly of most ponds liberally stocked with trout, is the fact that temperatures and seasons dictate strike zones. At times they will be on the surface and, again, deep down. If it's fly-fishing-only, then one is forced to operate with floating *and* fast-sinking lines. We never experienced any difficulty in reaching the proper levels, it was simply a matter of trial and error.

One day we were catching trout after trout on small wet flies and fast-sinking lines. We were fishing for fun, and some of our neighbors were not.

Presently a canoe containing two men and a woman closed in quietly. They were polite, as are most of Maine's citizens. "What the dickens are you fishin' for?"

"Trout," Whitney chuckled. "The place is alive with 'em."

"Aya, we see you catchin' trout, but you're throwin' 'em all back! What you usin' for bait?"

"A wet fly down deep," Charley explained. "A hairwing Royal Coachman. Use a sinking fly line and get it right down over the bottom."

"Don't you *want* those trout?"

"I want to catch 'em, and then I want to let 'em go," Whitney grinned—with which, having cast and let his line sink, he lifted the tip and played another magnificent little squaretail to net and released it. Our State of Maine friends shook their heads sadly and left us to our lunacy.

On Musquash Lake, again in central Maine, Arnold Laine boated an estimated 6-pound lake trout on a trolled Mooselook Wobbler. My brother, Dick, took a couple of pictures and then the togue was turned loose. That was standard operational procedure; we didn't want to eat the fish and there was no sense in wastage.

43

*Arnold Laine exhibits a Snake Pond, Maine, brook trout—
before the pond received heavy fishing pressure.*

Later, back at the landing, a French-Canadian lumberjack asked if we'd had any luck. Arnold said he'd caught a 5- or 6-pound laker and the woodsman asked to see it.

When Laine declared that he'd released the fish, our lumberjack guffawed, turned on his heel and stalked off. Such a thing was entirely beyond his comprehension.

Backwoodsmen are of two types. The first type, the majority, knows the water, is expert with pole or paddle, a canoe, or any other tool of the tall timber. Usually he is absolutely honest and hospitable. He can find his way, run rapids, make camp, cook delicious meals over a bed of coals—but he is a lousy fisherman. A minority of hinterlands types surprise you by having read all of the classics, hold degrees from reputable universities, and can not only quote Halford and Gordon but prove that they have mastered the art.

I'm going to make an observation that will be unpopular in the backcountry: the best and most scientific anglers in the world are residents of the great cities. There is good reason for this; city men have to fight like griffons to conquer a nearby wilderness where fish are hard to catch. They become supremely efficient since in no other way is it possible to succeed. The same thing applies in big-game hunting where the deadliest of marksmen is the city dweller who has trained on woodchucks with a scope-sighted rifle at 300 yards. That man is a perfectionist, because he has to be.

The truth goes beyond tradition and romance. For many years, we have extolled "Old Trapper Joe" and the legendary mountain men. We have thus brainwashed ourselves into believing that nobody but a backwoodsman can excel in hunting or fishing. That is nonsense, and it was always nonsense. The true expert has always been an intelligent, innovating invader, changing ancient strategies. The greatest handicap of a hinterlands resident is the belief that his tactics have always worked, so why change them when the going gets tough?

Anglers? I know a grizzled colleague who fishes culverts under country roads! He does almost nothing else, although he has sampled just about every rod and line sport in the world. Another friend is a scientific deep-troller, a master of wire line in the big lakes. He uses depth-sounders and a gimmick that charts trolling speed with or against the wind, plus an assortment of metal lures and streamer flies. There are spincasters who have progressed far beyond the "chuck it out and reel it in" school of thought.

The great thing about all of these specialists is the fact that they know all of the strategies on their own stamping grounds. All are foxy types who are virtuosos with bait, fly, spinning, or trolled offerings. Each weapons system is used where it is best suited to entice a trout, and top hands rarely bow to dogma. Never say "always," and never say "never," but don't get stuck into faddist opinion.

For example, contrary to popular opinion, successful wet fly and nymph presentation may be a far greater art than the use of a dry fly. If fish are rising and the water is broken, then the floating artificial can be sucker-bait. You fish it "up" or you fish it "down," and presenting a dry fly "as a living insect" was old stuff before grandfather cut his milk teeth. All you need is a properly balanced outfit and some skill in casting, plus a fly that is basically right sized and right colored. Nothing very revolutionary.

Or bait. At times there is nothing better than an angleworm —or part of an angleworm—a grasshopper, a cricket, a "perch bug," which is really a nymph seined out of a backwater, or maybe a grass shrimp imported from salt water, or a pinhead shiner. One uses each on proper tackle, and often the baiting gear challenges fly casting.

Trolling, either surface or deep, is an art in itself. The bad old boys who rack up record catches never learned their skills by reading, since there is little to read. They went out there and experimented, and some of their innovations will scare you. The best of them are scientific anglers who catch a lot of trout because they have worked out strategies that pay off when the rest of us are muttering about chubs in the humid evenings of July and August.

Lefty Kreh, famed for his fly-casting skill in both fresh and salt water, plays a Madison River, Montana, trout. (Photo by Lefty Kreh)

Of course we get into charges and countercharges. Some feel that anyone who angles for trout with anything other than a fly is strictly a meat fisherman. That's pretty silly because the specialist in each trade usually releases 90 percent of his catch. It is true that some baitmen kill everything, but one might argue that a healthy percentage of flycasters also murder every conquest.

Success means the number of trout raised, hooked, either kept or released. I have seen spincasters, trollers, and bait-fishermen tenderly return trout that an average feather-fancier would mount and hang on the wall. Also, I have seen supposedly gentle flycasters keep everything from tiddlers to trophies. Men are not catalogued by the tackle they employ.

In Canada, I watched a supposedly aristocratic angler throw dozens of sea-run brook trout up on the bank, to rot or be eaten by scavengers, because he felt that they endangered Atlantic salmon. On the Snake River in Wyoming I also witnessed the release of beautiful trout that were not desired for food.

Johnny Clark, an old friend, caught a trophy squaretail trout at the falls of Debsconeag in Maine. We had a few small ones for breakfast and civilization was too far away to warrant gifting. This was the largest squaretail Clark had ever caught in his life, but he handled it tenderly, made sure that we all witnessed his triumph, and then eased the regal creature back into its element. We never even took a picture.

Johnny Clark is a retired liquor dealer. He is unlikely to write a book, but he is an angling enthusiast as opposed to a senseless killer. He was skillful enough to catch a handsome trout, and man enough to let it go free in a green and gold wilderness where nobody knew, aside from his companions on that trip.

Some people *do* need to kill. There are countrymen who augment their larders in this age of spiraling food costs. I do not fault them, so long as the fish are honorably taken and consumed, and they do not engage in black market sale or waste. Compare the poor backwoodsman who collects a few illegal trout, salmon, or deer for sustenance with the millionaire industrialist who dams, pollutes, and kills entire rivers, clean-cuts timber so that nothing can live, or finances construction developments that murder all flora and fauna forever. Too often we embrace a double standard—and my sympathies are with the harried backwoods citizen.

American presidents go fishing, because it is expected of them, and some actually love the sport. Grover Cleveland was an enthusiast and Herbert Hoover liked nothing better than a few days of tranquillity far from the frustrations of high office. Once I blundered into an executive operation, and beat a hasty retreat.

Three of us were cruising the streams and ponds of Maine, and we went over to the Magalloway River. In that pristine wilderness there were police and plainclothesmen behind every tree. We finally braked to a halt and asked for an explanation. It seemed that Dwight Eisenhower, then President, was trout fishing on Parmachene.

I soldiered under Ike and I loved him as a supreme commander, but we reversed course and got the hell out of there. It would have been nice, I thought wistfully, if I could have spirited him out of that bee swarm of security agents and took him fishing in a better place. We wouldn't have fooled around with Parmachene and the overrated fly that bears its name.

We'd just have fished together, Ike and I, like old soldiers happy to be out in a whispering wilderness. We'd have caught a lot of trout and eaten good food flavored by the campfires. We'd probably even have shared a jug of Old Fuddlewit.

So, while Ike was squired royally and allowed to catch multitudes of stocked trout pumped into Parmachene, his ex-soldiers scooted right across the state and found some wonderful action with brown trout and landlocked salmon on dark little spider flies at Grand Lake Stream. Ike would have loved it, but rank has its responsibilities as well as its privileges. I don't think presidents have much fun.

Experts and anglers? The good ones may be Wall Street brokers or sweat-stained wilderness guides, plus characters who have been around since creation and have learned everything there is to know. Although I hate to admit it, outdoor writers are questionable. In this business you'd better study the man in action, not his professional credits, color, creed, and zeal.

An expert *and* an angler is the gentleman who can put it all together on a fishing ground.

4

The Untouchables

Let purists smile wanly and lift their patrician noses: I simply want to see the brother-in-blood who can cast a fly to a trout nestled under a hummock in an icy trickle guarded by a latticework of tangled willows and dead brush—a place where there is no opportunity to false-cast because of the surrounding jungle, where a pool may be no more than a tiny, gouged-out hole under a cut bank, *under* a canopy of wild grapevines so thick that a water snake would have to consult some built-in compass to arrive at a given point.

To use a fly in a brush-choked brook is nothing short of lunacy. There, if you would be successful in landing the tiny, jewel-tinted beauties that have never seen a state hatchery, you must go to bait artfully presented. It will be close-range work, but never clumsy meat-fishing. There will be just as much expertise exhibited as ever displayed by a master angler offering a tiny dry fly on a crystal limestone stream.

A great bait-fisherman may be the most expert of anglers. Only a few really succeed and these, more often than not, are aces who have conquered all of the methods, only to find that clever baiting is a supreme challenge. The nonpareils are secre-

Bait fishing a Massachusetts pond can be a deadly method when fish aren't feeding at the surface.

tive, since they engage in an art that our literature apparently condemns with much talk of artificial flies and a put-down of bait as the weapon of a poacher, or worse.

The sole trouble with bait is that it is the first choice of a beginner. The tyro feels that fish feed on angleworms and shiners, so that is what he uses on the saddest of tackle. Delicacy of presentation is ignored and, since there is too little in the literature to digest and implement, our aspirant has few champions to admire and emulate. He is a lone wolf, sure that something is wrong with the business, but uncertain. There may even be a guilt feeling, fostered by years of exposure to learned works on fly casting for trout, each sneering at the use of natural bait.

This is unfortunate. Often bait is the only effective killer, and anyone who denies this displays ignorance. Although I prefer the fly, I tip my hat to colleagues who can readily switch from one technique to another as conditions demand. Moreover, I like to fish with bait when that is most effective. Unfortunately, I have a tendency to use natural fodder only in a small and jungle-bordered stream. I am wrong.

There are, in this land of ours, thousands upon thousands of cold rivulets that support native trout. These are not big fish, but they are fun and they are delicious table fare. Such marvelous creations live in trickles coursing through tangled swamps and mountain bogs. If you want to take them, you must be a hunter as well as a fisherman—and you'd best adopt specialized tactics. I see nothing wrong with this.

Certainly a schoolboy or a bumbler of any age will slam a gob of worms into a pool and hope that, after the miniature tidal wave subsides, a trout will "nibble." A few victims fall for these tactics, but most of them are the hatchery stupids just dumped in by a yawning employee of the resident Division of Fisheries and Game, who is stocking pools nearest state roads and wondering, vaguely, if he can get rid of those fin-clipped "catchables" quickly enough to hide for a few hours in the nearest tavern.

It's different with wild, native trout, or even with those that have survived the hatchery plagues and learned to feast on stream fodders after a couple of weeks of aimless wandering. Now, either wild spawn or acclimated, you get fish that spook at a shadow or a vibration on the bank, trout that are wary of a crude presentation of an unnaturally bunched bait. All of the losers conclude that a stream is "fished out," and call a friend in the Division of Fisheries and Game to ask where the latest load has been dumped. The following of hatchery trucks is no humorous myth; it is a way of life for jugheads who never learned to fish.

Skilled baiters are close-mouthed secretive folk who know every turn and curve and undercut bank in the little brooks. They know that trout are there and that they must be outfoxed by a quiet approach and skillful presentation. There are basic rules.

First, stealth. Approach each pool or run as though stalking a particularly sharp-eyed enemy scout. Hold bankside vibration to an absolute minimum. Wear neutral-colored or camouflage clothing that will blend into the background, and never present a silhouette against a wide, blue sky. Never, but never, let your shadow fall over a pool or any part of it.

Small-stream fishing, like the hunting of grouse in hot corners, improves with familiarity. Each brook has its own secret runs and pools, each its idiosyncrasies dependent on water conditions. Roughly a microcosm of big rivers, a tiny trickle presents added difficulties: first, one battles the brush, the trembling banks, and, almost certainly, mosquitoes, black flies, and no-see-ums. Second, trout banquet halls must literally be stumbled upon (or fallen into) because they are well camouflaged by a tangle of swamp growth.

On a well-pounded brook close to a metropolitan city, I could show you a veritable sure thing for trout, if I were inclined to do so. It lies smack-dab in the middle of a tremendous bower of wild Concord grapevines, completely hidden and always bypassed by the multitudes who come stomping along, plopping worm-baited hooks into open runs.

If I pinpointed the location, yet offered no operational plan of attack, it would still require some time to discover the secret. There is absolutely no way to drift a bait into that pothole because it is not only guarded by a formidable tangle of sunken vines, but because it lies at the very tail of a shallow dead water. The trick is to lower a tempting morsel through a small opening in the very center of that incredible brushpile: it arrives at a point where a slight and sluggish current pulses into a dark, cold, and deep kettle.

Properly executed, and assuming that no immediate predecessor has tried to wade through the vines and go over his boot tops and flounder wildly, the maneuver is immediately greeted by a solid take. One then attempts to derrick a writhing, junior-grade trophy up through the grapevines. Some, ill-handled, will succeed in looping around a stem below, yet there is little difficulty if you "keep him coming." A small trout on a proper hook is a very slick and streamlined customer indeed.

Another stream, unstocked for decades, intrigues a close-mouthed few of us because it is amazingly productive at one time, and one time only. This brook meanders down out of highland springs, through swale swamp, under a trunk highway, and finally empties into a pond of middling size. There are the usual pools buried in jungle growth, and you won't catch a bloody thing on beautiful mornings and afternoons when all conditions suggest ideal trout fishing.

Here, it is wise to plan an attack immediately after any hard spring shower while water levels are rising so rapidly that one thinks of tides. For some curious reason, perhaps because they are running up from the pond in a spate, squaretails engage in a feeding spree. Most of them, as is the norm in a tiny stream, measure 8 to 10 inches, yet a friend of mine who was working a midget worm chunk in a pool he could have jumped across the day before came up with a 2½-pound brookie.

It was a hell of a battle on 2-pound test monofilament, and therefore something of a miracle when Warren Williams of Worcester, Massachusetts, finally led his prize close enough to scoop in a hand net. Fat, deep-bodied, and as gloriously colored as the brookies that Daniel Webster caught while he wasn't proving his skill as an orator (and his frustration at the elusiveness of the Presidency), this fish was no spawn of the hatcheries.

The point is, a master of small-stream angling must know his favorite ground like a red fox knows his territory. A first trip to any unfamiliar brook may be reasonably successful, yet the primary mission is prospecting, learning just where and how a bank is undercut or a moldering log provides natural cover. Often the bonanzas are difficult to reach with a baited hook, so there must be time for prior reconnaissance.

Bob Williams, Warren's brother, is skilled in all of the angling arts from salt water through fresh, but he gets his big

Bob Williams removes fly from a heavy squaretail trout in north-central Maine.

kicks by taking native trout from roadside culverts and brooks never stocked. Part of the challenge is a proven ability to collect handsome little squaretails from trickles that are ignored by the multitudes who pass them daily, grimly speeding to larger streams promoted by the Division of Fisheries and Game.

Bob uses a "filleted worm," and admirers declare that one nightcrawler is all he needs for a day of fishing. Using ultralight tackle and tiny claw hooks, he really does nothing but present the marine troller's strip-bait in miniature. It is a very deadly method if you are craftsman enough to hook and play the fancy little warriors on 2-pound test line and limber fly rod.

Equipment includes a light, maybe 7 ½ foot, soft-action rod; an enclosed spool spinning reel easily controlled with an index finger; a very light monofilament line, about 4-pound test at maximum—and that is a bit heavy for best results. Carry a sharp knife and a few angleworms for bait. No leader. Bend a size 12 claw-type hook to the end of the mono.

Now "fillet a worm" (it isn't true filleting because you will simply cut a portion of a squirmer, using a segment one-half to three-quarters of an inch long). Impale this offering on the point of the hook so that it will stream naturally in any current or upon the retrieve. Work the bait downstream, feeding it into the hidey-holes. Bring it back slowly, twitching the rod tip to create action.

Trout, contrary to some popular opinion, can scent (or perhaps taste) anything good to eat. The cut worm segment streams natural juices and it also flutters enticingly. A solid strike usually means a hooked fish and, even with a tiny barb, that trout will be snagged well forward in the mouth so that it can be released.

Tackle for trickles has evolved over the years, and the most popular combination includes a light, soft, medium-length fly rod, the sort of thing we used to tout as a 2- to 3-ounce wet-fly action calibrated to HDH before the Numbers Boys emerged. Snakes are better than light ring guides.

Use a neat little slip-cast reel featuring a smooth drag and absolute line control. While an open-face type can be used, its whirling cone of line is a brush-catcher and there is greater difficulty in operation when one must live-line free mono in a current. Any ordinary single-action fly reel is efficient and may even be superior when an angler finds it most comfortable. I like single-action but, much as I hate to admit it, the better performers gravitate to slip-cast.

Nothing other than nylon monofilament will do, and it should be as light as is practical under the circumstances. Anything over 6-pound test is too heavy. Four is better and, if you can handle it, 2-pound test is supreme. We used to work with enameled fly lines, and then the plastic-coated varieties, but all are trouble-prone in a veritable woodcock jungle because they are too bulky for the swift steering of a light bait. In addition, with a standard fly line, a leader must be attached—and that is a connection that grabs floating debris or grass. The one redeeming feature of a fly line is the fact that you can switch back and forth between bait and flies as the situation requires.

In my opinion, nothing beats the Eagle Claw hook for baiting. Size, however, is a thing you have to determine on site. Obviously, a very tiny bait, like the filleted worm, is unlikely to fare well if presented on a large barb, and there are other baits that simply cannot be fished with reasonable success on a husky grapnel. These include salmon eggs, "perch bugs," the nymphs of various stream insects, pinhead shiners, and such exotics as tiny translucent grass shrimp. Tailor the hook to the bait and don't worry about holding power; you are not fishing for tuna.

The hook is tremendously important in all sportfishing, fresh or salt. Curiously, people will spend vast amounts on rods, reels, lines, and other equipment, then try to economize on a hook that costs pennies. Insist on the best and carry a selection of different sizes. Hone them sharp—and then still sharper!

Bait serves the purpose in larger streams, even in densely populated suburban areas.

Trout Hunting

One charge against baiters, levied by fly-fishermen, is the undeniable fact that live fodder often means deep hooking and subsequent injury to the trout so that it cannot be released. This rarely happens with the worm strip, where hooking is swift, or with natural nymphs, grasshoppers, or shrimp. It does apply in the use of pickled salmon eggs and there is no escaping the charge when one, two, or a gob of angleworms on a small hook requires swallowing before a strike is prudent.

There are occasions when one or two whole worms, carefully threaded on a hook so that they stream in the currents and appear engaged in the business of copulation, will be highly successful. At this time a step upward in hook size is a conservation measure that does not ensure defeat. Instead of a size 8 or 6, go to a 4 or even a 2. Then the jeweled midgets of the small streams will be hooked well forward and can be released with ease. If they are stupid enough to grab a gob of worms, then they won't be spooked by a big barb.

On a small and brush-bound stream, this is the most efficient gear. However, there is a reason sometimes for snake guides on a fly rod, instead of light rings. There will be occasions when some trickle widens out into meadow pools where trout are taking flies and scorning bait. Carry a single-action reel loaded with the suitable line and tapered leader. It takes scant moments to switch, and you're in business. Either snakes or rings will do, but the latter are heavier and less versatile.

So far as rod types and materials are concerned, there was a good argument for the ancient telescoping steel shaft: it could be swiftly proportioned for a job at hand, such as poking a small bait into a screened kettle, or lobbing where that was necessary. Its shortcomings were its brute strength and excess weight where true sport depended on delicacy.

Split bamboo is fine, yet nobody needs a Paine, a Leonard, or an Orvis here. In fact, it may be something of sacrilege to battle the bushes with a classic wand of great price and pedigree. Tubular fiberglass is ideal, low in price compared to the

The author uses fluorescent yellow monofilament line to steer a bait through the clutching brush guarding a tiny stream.

custom split bamboo, tougher, more efficient. If the name of the game is success, there is no comparison.

Similarly, advanced monofilament lines are inexpensive, easy to use, and better than any other strand in the close-range operation. Popular tints may or may not be important. A majority prefers something as near transparent as possible, while others like mist blue, light green, or amber.

Intrigued by duPont's development of a fluorescent yellow monofilament, I experimented with it in fresh water and salt. There is, one must understand, a far-from-new theory expounded by scientists from Germany, Russia, and the United States, that many game fish "see as through a yellow lens." Therefore, I acquired some of the neon-tinted yellow mono from duPont and proceeded to test it on small stream trout. As a control, I called in Bob Williams who, as previously mentioned, is an expert in the art of snaking natives out of trickles.

Regardless of whether a fish can or cannot see a yellow line because it views the world through a butter-colored filter, there is one thing going for this activated strand: the angler can see the line! In small-stream baiting one must steer a tempter through an assortment of malicious snags, often in poor light. The fluorescent glows and so it is easily guided. That is an advantage in itself.

We started, and this was four years ago, with 10-pound test and found it too heavy for practical work. Admittedly, we launched the project by using a translucent leader tippet because we thought that no trout could stomach a line that looked like a bar of neon. Initially, the idea was a strand that could be steered past the usual clutching clumps of brush.

Then we went to 6-pound test, and *that* was a triumph. Trout—brookie, brown, and rainbow—were swiftly reduced to possession. There was no need of a transparent leader, for they seemed to disregard the brilliant color. Later, after duPont made me a special run of 4-pound test golden fluorescent Stren, it was even better. We could see the line, and the trout, evidently, could not. It was a grand step forward in bait fishing.

Now duPont is marketing yellow string in the light tests, yet it remains almost unknown, the secret weapon of a few specialists who are imaginative enough to shrug off dogma and try something new. The stuff is not readily available, since a lot of dealers are unwilling to stock line that is not in steady demand.

It *is* new, and it *is* good. Edwin H. Keller, recently retired as duPont's chief of plastic fishing lines, provided me with early extrusions that I used and then farmed out to local experts who were admittedly skeptical. The line worked so well that I had a steady succession of advanced bait-fishermen

Dick Woolner snakes a miniature brookie out of a meadow stream that he has approached on hands and knees.

visiting my office to ask for free spools of the yellow mono they couldn't buy locally. Now the fluorescents are available in all tests and I am inclined to think that they will become important in fly casting, too.

Most of us too often jump to conclusions, but pioneers take their lumps and wade in—they ride to win and take full ad-

Paul Kukonen displays an Arctic char landed away up in Canada's precambrian shield.

vantage of every technological advance. It is wise to forget classic tradition when it is proved lacking, to ignore old-crock belief and nonsensical promotion. There are no miracles, but there is honest progress. A sense of humor helps.

Paul Kukonen, a highly erudite angling friend who runs a sporting-goods shop, has a weird mind. A local, who must be a remittance man because he fishes every day during the course of a season, one day arrived to complain that he was catching nothing but dace—and the dace were getting smaller and smaller. It was mid-August.

Dead-pan, Kukonen said: "Don't you know that the 'dace' get shorter and shorter after June 21?"

He said the guy never even cracked a smile, but turned on his heel and stalked out. I advised Paul that the man must have been abnormal, else he'd have whupped out a gaff and stuck him right through the gizzard!

There are baits—and *baits*. Angleworms are always cited because they are traditional. While few think of such refinements as ultralight tackle and common, yet somehow exotic, offerings, the masters embrace science and thereby enjoy sport while their friends go hungry.

Armed with some little knowledge of aquatic natural history, it is no great thing to devise seines that will catch hellgrammites and a variety of nymphs—some of them big enough to scare a grown man. Pinhead shiners can be devastating, and sometimes mummichogs, called "killifish" by Long Island types, are better than spun gold. Crickets, grasshoppers, and even cockroaches have proved highly effective. A few grand old brown trout have been reduced to possession via a live frog or a swimming mouse pinned by the neck and forced to breast the currents. (I am against this: the mouse, the frog, and I are too closely allied in the chain of creation.)

Grasshoppers and crickets are more easily utilized, although I have a personal fondness for the latter, since they are friends who shrill in my cellar office through the winter. Grasshoppers are stupids who never consort with mankind, but only hop, fly, and drool "tobacco juice" in the long noonings of summer. Serves 'em right.

With either grasshoppers or crickets, both exceptionally good baits, you employ light-end tackle, primarily because nothing else will do. The chitinous shell of these insects demands a small and almost weightless hook, carefully placed. Salamanders and newts are secret weapons in some localities, particularly where trout are large. There are, in addition, a whole host of grubs and bee larvae, all more attractive to a game fish than a common angleworm.

Pickled or fresh, natural in color or dyed to various fluorescent shades, a single salmon egg on a tiny hook—in turn bent to a spiderweb line—can be mighty deadly. Most small-stream trout have never seen a salmon egg in their brief life spans, yet they have some built-in sixth sense for that which is good to eat. This leads to another point—the true exotic.

Back in the days when miniature grass shrimp were considered ne plus ultra as chum and bait for common weakfish along the North Atlantic coast, tackle and bait shops 100 miles inland would stock them for sale to hungries headed seaward. Inevitably, a few trout addicts decided to try the little kickers on browns, rainbows, and squaretails.

They worked like grease! Certainly these inland tiddlers had never seen or tasted a marine shrimp, but they pounced on each one adequately presented. The answer probably lies in scent; while unfamiliar, the shrimp smelled like Thanksgiving morning to a hungry trout.

There are things no gentleman will do—and yet do anyway! I cannot raise a fever over baits like whole kernel corn, bits of marshmallow, lumps of processed cheese, and doughballs. All, on occasion, are attractive to trout.

Whole kernel corn is an unlikely natural bait, yet it works. Some say that trout gorge on the stuff when used as chum, and then die. The same charge was made of extensive corn chumming for flounders in marine waters, but a research project in 1973 proved this a fallacy. Flounders stuffed with a 50 percent diet of the grain over a period of months not only lived happily but gained weight. Chumming is rarely done in small streams, so the growls of purists are valid only in that such tiny baits usually ensure deep hooking and subsequent destruction of the quarry.

Sometimes corn kernels appear to be the only baits trout devour avidly—especially recently stocked fish—so this creates new flights of fancy. Paul Belton, a friend who likes to fish with a fly and who manages a club pool, got all upset when his beautifully tied artificials were ignored in favor of the Golden Bantam deluge, so he went home and whipped up a batch of corn flies. These were nothing but a few turns of yellow chenille on a size 14 hook, but the things worked. You just cast them out there and let them sink. Bang! In business.

A few years back when I was writing a daily newspaper rod and gun column, one springtime season found doughballs enjoying considerable favor. I reported the phenomenon and dubbed the bait "Pillsbury Hackle."

There was, at that time, an excellent local tackle shop presided over by a talented gent named Earl Mineau and his lovely German-born wife. She sported a delightful accent, plus wide-eyed astonishment at the demands of American anglers. One day when I visited, Frau Mineau's blue eyes were sparking like those of a Prussian general planning all-out attack.

She raged. "Gott knows I haff tried! I haff learned *all* of zese American flies, but zey keep asking for somezing zere iss not! *Vot* is dot Pillsbury Hackle?"

A good deal of small-stream baiting is educated live-lining with no terminal weight to take the offering down. However, when a stream is in spate or you are fishing a fast run that dumps into a deeper hole, then the addition of one or two split-shot often ensures success. I hold the BB size range best, and the shape is right because a sphere is less likely to foul than a wrap of strip lead.

Bait fishing in big water does not appeal to me, even though I know it can be high art and have been outmaneuvered time and again by smirking brothers in arms who get down into the strike zone while I am fooling around with flies in upper, desert levels.

A majority of pond fishermen lack skill—they granny-knot a frighteningly large hook to the end of a coarse leader, add a fist-sized bunch of nightcrawlers, attach a sinker large enough to hold bottom in a riptide, and heave the whole mess out there. Don't curse them, the lads are conservationists. Rather, look out for a minority of perfectionists who study their quarry, deliberate about bottom conformation, evaluate temperature, thermocline, and bait. These characters decimate trout.

Almost always the perfectionists are light-tackle enthusiasts, often graduates of spin and fly who get a thrill from boating eyebrow-raising trophies while the purists mumble about hot weather, too many water skiers, pollution, a lack of adequate stocking, or simply declare that "the pond is fished out." The dainty classicists are wrong, and they know that they are wrong. If trout are away down in the depths it is a journey into frustration to flail the shallows. You go to deep trolling or to bait on the bottom in high summer. Let's see: are you a master trout hunter, or just another specialist in a single discipline?

Lakes and ponds usually host larger trout than the minor streams, yet this is the place for ultralight tackle while baiting. There is a need for fine lines, plus sophisticated hooks and other goodies. Chumming can be extremely effective and, of course, there must be an awareness of depth and bottom con-formation. Season is important, because each month of the year finds trout in different locations. Come July and August, the husky rainbow or brown of springtime will desert the shallows and haunt deep, cold depths where smelt live a pre-carious existence.

Baits differ from those used in feeder streams, primarily because the fish are larger and therefore feed on a host of morsels that would scare the little, glittering beauties. There are exceptions, which will be noted, but most of the carnage is accomplished with live shiners, smelt, chubs, sucker fry, and cut baits taken from all of these. As usual, of course, the artfully presented angleworm or nightcrawler accounts for trout, if only because squirmers are most often employed.

In the beginning of it, after ice-out and a corresponding plenitude of cold, well-oxygenated water at the surface, shallow waters produce. The old-timers, those who know their quarry and can almost hear the grass grow, move to locations adjacent to stream mouths. If there is a spawning run of smelt under way, so much the better. In these locations the water is *alive*, pulsing, carrying all sorts of food down into a lake. Smorgasbords are appreciated by both men and trout.

Later, as the season mellows and surface temperatures warm, then trout course deep. They are taken in numbers only by deep trollers, flycasters who emerge in the deep night hours, and by hooded-eyed old bait fishermen who anchor over the deep holes.

Go down deep or you will enjoy a water haul with much sunlight, birdsong, tranquillity—and very few fish to brag about. Use monofilament line and make it light. Heavy gear is an abomination in a goldfish bowl; it is unnecessary and it spooks game fish because it hampers the natural movement of bait. Go to light and limber rods, designed to cushion rather than to stop a determined lunge. Think about sinkers just heavy enough to get that tempter into a strike zone, and choose hooks created for a specific purpose, usually short-shanked types, as small as is practical.

Hook a shiner, a smelt, or a live chub through the top of the nose or through the skin just ahead of the dorsal fin—and the latter is better because the creature will live longer. String an angleworm sparingly, so that it will squirm. Bury a hook in any soft cut bait. Fish with free-spool and don't get excited about a nibble or an initial short run. With any sizable bait, the deep-down trout is likely to take gingerly, then run for a short distance prior to turning the offering and swallowing

Bruce Woolner, author's nephew, beams over a catch of native squaretails.

it head first. Let him pause to turn the bait, to gulp it, and to start another little run. Now sock it to him; unless he's a midget, he'll be on.

The Untouchables

There is one deadly method I do not recommend, and for one reason. The method is the deep-down operation with salmon eggs and either egg or whole-kernel corn chumming. It is highly effective after springtime has melted into summer and the surface temperatures are winding up. Then you find trout in the holes and they are patsies on the proper bait presented on ultralight tackle and miniature hooks. Corn kernels may do, but pickled salmon eggs are better. With either, the hook should be a tiny, gold-plated claw, the sort of thing a flycaster would consider right for a spider pattern.

I see nothing horrendous about the technique, other than the fact that a corn kernel or salmon egg usually is gulped down well before any hook is set. If an angler wants a limit catch and takes the first that come to net, that's all right. Unfortunately, since trophy trout are so often seduced by egg or kernel, a meat-man is tempted to release those that fail to attain bragging size. Again all right, except that the deeply lodged barb may mean the demise of a trout.

Much has been made of the theory that rusting and corrosion will eliminate a hook from the mouth, or even the gullet, of a game fish. Perhaps, but now we use stainless-steel hardware and it is pretty obvious that the ripping of gills ensures speedy death. Hungries who return fish after fish, regardless of hurt, until they have their limits of lunkers contribute to the destruction of a sacred natural resource.

This is a sin difficult to pinpoint, and the harried game wardens cannot cope with it. Lacking first-hand observation and proof, who can tell whether a released fish is mortally wounded or fit as the proverbial fiddle? Some jokers like to bait wardens and I know one character who did so solely for laughs. On this occasion trolled flies were the weapons, so there were no casualties.

His name is Leo Perry and he is a magnificent trout fisherman. One day, working a well-stocked pond from a small boat and scoring steadily, he noticed a minion of the law back at the launching ramp. The lad with a Smokey Bear hat had binoculars, so Leo quietly caught trout after trout, consigning each to a light canvas bag slung around his waist. He caught some forty or fifty before cranking up and heading for home.

The warden intercepted, as planned by both parties, and asked to see that bag. There was nothing in it, other than a gaping hole in the bottom. Leo had contrived to hold the container over the gunwale as he inserted each lively trout. All had gone free and healthy because Perry doesn't give a damn for dead fish. It is to the lawman's credit that he laughed and admitted himself flummoxed.

Perry is one of those perfectionists who knows all of the tricks, and he fishes with everything that works. Leo assaulted striped bass in the years immediately after World War II and he became a "regular," which—in the vernacular of beachcombers—means that he was one of the best. Nobody could top him, but he went back to inland trout because he felt there was greater challenge. The man is an incomparable fisherman and has an explosive scorn for people who "talk fishing," but have not been there, for status folk and writers who research in libraries instead of slogging back in the bush where success is measured by individual expertise.

I cite Perry only because he is the complete, aboriginal angler—no purist, no seeker of medals. Most important is the fact that Perry is more an authority than many of the poohbahs. He has sampled it all, salt and fresh. He can tie nymphs you wouldn't believe, and every one is an exact copy of something he dredged out of pond or stream. He is a superb flycaster, yet he employs bait where that is necessary—and the operation is as carefully planned as the incision of a brain surgeon. He loves trout, so he releases ten for every one kept.

Great bait fishermen are anglers who have come full circle. First, there was the bumbling effort of youth, the heavy tackle and the well-weighted nightcrawler. Next, an expedition into fly casting with all of its suborders of wet, dry, nymph, streamer, and terrestrial. Then spinning, light and heavy; then deep and shallow trolling, with all of the gimmicks and aids.

All of it is good and all of it is nice, but a master often returns to one of the greatest challenges of all—bait on a fine line. It may not be status, but it is high art. Some of us forget that our patron saint, Isaac Walton, was a bait fisherman.

There is nothing obscene about it, yet there *is* some stain on the souls of lesser men who cannot master the science and therefore consign it to limbo, autocratically condemning a skill they have never attained.

This is sacrilege, and I know it—and I don't care because it is true. I have fished with every tackle combination across most of our hemisphere, and I prefer to use flies. But, if I had to catch trout for a living, then I would go to bait at all seasons. Almost always a well-presented natural is far better than any artificial.

Sorry, but that's the way it is. Would you like the usual nonsense, or do you want the facts of the matter?

5

Spinning,
the New Faith

It is probable that more trout are now taken on spinning tackle than on any other sportfishing combination. This stirs the bile of brothers who feel that use of hardware is a short step up from angleworms, and it is commonly held that no gentleman descends to either. In the interest of accuracy, note that this is a minority opinion.

In 1973, Norman Strung and Milt Rosko collaborated on a book titled *Spinfishing*. A subtitle declares: *The System That Does It All*. It's a fine work, although I must admit to a rather startled double take. Then I thought—maybe they have an argument! Fixed-spool *can* do it all. Not well, but nobody said *that*.

Spinning tackle can be used to throw artificial lures, or fish bait on the bottom; it can be pressed into service on the trolling grounds, and it will cast flies—if fitted with a bubble float or a sinker to provide casting weight. Just possibly this is the nearest thing to an all-round outfit ever designed, even though it is supremely efficient in a few basic tasks, such as the casting of miniature metal and plastic lures or the presentation of featherweight natural baits.

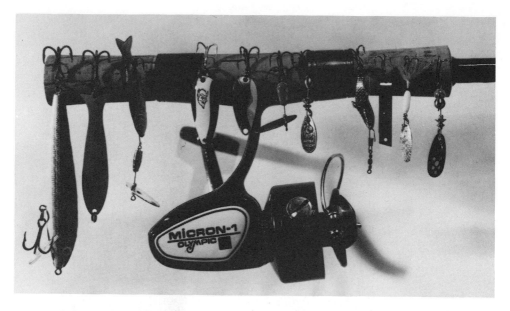

Ultralight spinning tackle can be highly efficient in trout fishing, and lures range all the way from miniature plugs on up through featherweight wobblers, spoons, and spinners. For best results, lines in the 2- to 4-pound-test bracket complement this system.

In America we mistakenly think fixed-spool a new idea. Actually, this theory goes back to antiquity when certain savage gentlemen wound lines around rude spools and then cast baits by turning the axis of the spool toward a mark. It was early heave and haul, but it surely prevented tangles.

In the mid-1880s, Peter Malloch of Perth, Scotland, fashioned an advanced model—yet it was far from practical. Later, in 1920, England's Holden Illingworth produced the forerunner of all modern spinning reels. This one featured gearing, an enclosed housing, and a bail. The system gained favor in Europe, but wasn't introduced to America until 1935 when Bache Brown pioneered its use in the United States.

Russell Tinsley wrestles a Montana trout on fixed-spool. (Photo by Russell Tinsley)

Brown fought an uphill battle. There was sales resistance to overcome, plus the scorn of flycasters and baitcasters who felt their systems adequate. Then, of course, World War II set the planet on fire and guns were more important than fishing tackle. Spinning really made its American debut in 1946 when dozens of imports were made available and a few U.S. concerns saw the wave of the future. A few of these early reels were excellent, most were unmitigated junk.

I never saw a spinning reel until 1944 when, in touring Europe with a group of colleagues in tin hats, I confiscated a couple of French abortions made of hard plastic—toted by German soldiers on their way back to the fatherland by way of a POW camp. Finally discharged and back in America manning a fishing rod and a typewriter instead of a 90mm cannon, some manufacturer gifted me with a neat little spinning outfit on the eve of a trip into the backcountry. I don't recall who made the rig, and it doesn't matter because that firm has long been out of business. The reel had an egg-shaped gear housing made of anodized aluminum and it was, in retrospect, a fine piece of equipment. There was a medium-priced, but decent, split-bamboo spinning rod as well, plus a few lures. At the time I recall feeling that my own light-casting artificials would work better—things like miniature Dardevles, for instance.

Four of us followed topo maps, bumping over a tote road into a little campsite on a strictly wilderness river where we launched a pair of tin boats and tooled up into a remote little lake through a hidden thoroughfare. It was a place well populated with squaretail trout and some landlocked salmon, the shoreline was always punctuated by bear tracks, and often you'd see a cow moose.

Each of us took turns with the new foreign devil, and it sure caught fish—but we hated it.

Okay, we were confirmed flycasters armed with good split-bamboo rods and single-action reels. Like so many Americans at that time we were sure that just two outfits were worthy of applause, the fly-casting and the bait-casting combinations, with a stiff little bow to marine surf and offshore rigs which, in our exalted opinion, were nothing more than beefed-up bait-casting and heavy conventional trolling outfits.

Our quartet, unfortunately, never gave spinning a fair shake. I used the tackle for a while, duty-bound, and my companions essayed a few casts. We then decided that fixed spool was an European abomination. To us it was awkward, troublesome to reel with the left hand, a sorry stranger in paradise. True, a number of squaretails and a few salmon belted Dardevles, yet in that place and at that time, it was easy to believe that you could take them on anything.

Probably the outfit was far ahead of its time, featuring a simple reel with a smooth drag coupled to a sensitive rod. Our error was to summarily dismiss it and go right back to flinging flies.

Fixed-spool tackle is highly efficient, as I have found in the long years since. Good books have been written about the art, among them works by Al McClane and Joe Bates, in addition to the recent, aforementioned book by Norm Strung and Milt Rosko. Bache Brown, of course, was one of the first boosters.

Brown really brought it to America, and Bates blew the bugle. The two lived in Longmeadow, Massachusetts, and they got together. Bache, according to Joe, copied the Pezon-Michel French spinning reel and produced it in Springfield. "He had parts made by different firms, and none of them fitted together until he did some handwork on them, to end up with reels that worked—barely! He sold out to Airex, which went down the spout after a year or so. Then Gaston Mieg got hold of me and wanted me to help him promote the Ru series of spinning reels, Tortue mono, and C. P. Swing lures. Gaston and I were very close friends. We tested tackle in Florida and other areas, and the Ru reels were tops for many years."

Bates declares that the surf-stick types still used were developed "by Gaston and me. We had the Montague Rod

*This Alaskan rainbow couldn't resist a metal spinning lure.
(Photo by Russell Tinsley)*

Frank Woolner with landlock caught on a spinning lure.

Company make samples and, naturally, they put them in their line without paying us a cent. Other manufacturers copied them. Of course, they were bamboo then, but the glass sticks now used are very similar."

Joe Bates was certainly one of America's pioneers in the promotion of spinning, an art that he admits has faults, but one that has started millions of people fishing.

These chroniclers—and Al McClane was right in there with inspired literature—detailed a new art, but some of them forgot a mighty important point. Spinning came to America as a foreign devil and was long suspect. Then, because it was promoted as all-purpose, free of backlash, a foolproof technique, legions of citizens rushed to buy.

Initial concepts are so ludicrous that one must wonder at the mentality capable of accepting nonsense. Spinning is not all-purpose and it is far from foolproof. There are no "backlashes," but that is a matter of semantics because there are horrendous line sloughs that can be worse than any time-honored bird's nest. The reels are still delicate, compared to revolving-spool, and too easily rendered unserviceable. There are problems with sticky drags and accident-prone bail springs, the latter necessary in light-line casting where a lure must be started back immediately after touchdown. Automatic bails have been devised, but few have won acclaim other than in salt water. The manual bail is almost entirely a marine-fishing option.

No matter. Any human being with the normal complement of fingers and reflexes can learn to use spinning tackle in minutes. This neophyte will not be an advanced angler after brief instruction, but he will be able to throw it out and bring it back. *And he will catch fish.*

Most important, spinning has become the open sesame to sportfishing. Having begun with this amazingly efficient, although erroneously proclaimed all-purpose system, the thoughtful angler branches out. In addition to fixed-spool, he goes to fly rods and bait-casting rods, advanced trolling out-

Spinning tackle is often made to order for big trout. Emil Casey of West Brookfield, Massachusetts, caught this 18-pound 7-ounce brown in nearby Quabbin Reservoir. He was casting from shore.

fits, and the deadly little combinations that are so good in small-stream baiting. In brief, the experimenting man becomes an advanced angler.

Sorrowful indeed are the legions who never progress; they start with fixed-spool and continue to believe that this is the only method. Such zealots cannot understand that spinning is supreme in its sphere of efficiency but sadly lacking elsewhere. Those who stubbornly cling to the fixed-spool display abysmal ignorance. They are blood brother to the status dry-fly purist and the harmless nut who think that any game fish on land or sea can be subdued with a single outfit.

But it just doesn't work that way—we need several weapons systems.

Roughly, spinning reels fall into two categories: open-face and closed-face. There are all sorts of variations, some of them promising for specialized operations and combining the thumb control of revolving-spool with the easy slip-cast operation of true spinning. All serve a purpose.

Open-face is less trouble-prone than closed-face, and for several reasons. First, there is no shielding hood to confine running line and prevent immediate correction when a line snarls in that bastardly bird's nest called a "line slough," instead of a backlash. (Of course professional baitcasters *never* have backlashes—they suffer "over-run.") Similarly, if through butter-fingered handling you break off a fish, then that is a "long-line release." Recently I started to read a book by a self-appointed bait-casting authority. In the first chapter he declared that he never suffered backlash, and that's where I quit reading.

A closed-face spinning reel can be iced up in cold weather, and it can be plagued by unseen corrosion. If, after a break off, you inadvertently reel that end of line through the little hole in the end of the hood, then it takes time to disassemble the winch and put it back together.

Because advanced anglers prefer open-face, most of the closed-face types are cheaply constructed and therefore prone to short life (a few are excellent and can be highly efficient for certain tasks). Actually, nothing really beats a good closed-face fixed-spool reel where the angler desires to combine light natural bait fishing with the tossing of miniature lures in small water. I think nothing is better for baiting in a small stream, and for the occasional use of hardware on such a ground.

Too many of the closed-face types are manufactured to sell at a pittance. These cheapies are junk, and it is well to realize that inexpensive open-face reels are just as short-lived. The interminable copies, short cuts, and bargains are often quite bad. They won't work well when new; they break down rapidly and you can't buy parts. It's far better to lay out a few more dollars and purchase the leader of a recognized firm that will stand behind its product.

Initially, for an angler trained in other disciplines, the concept of left-hand drive is unsettling. (Fixed-spool reels with right-hand drive are readily available, but hardly popular.) You can beat this easily; in fact, an average angler soon finds a measure of ambidextrous ability. It is a good thing, because the spinning outfit is two handed. The index finger of the right hand releases and guides or feathers the line, while the left hand carefully takes up slack and cranks while pumping—and never against a running drag because this will ensure line twist. Twist, incidentally, is another Achilles' heel of every spinning reel.

Drag settings are confusing. First, if a reel is well machined, then it will feature a very smooth, adjustable drag. It should be silk smooth, not jerky, and then it must be set to proper tension. You'll need a "striking drag," which is just about enough to set the hook. Beyond that, it is folly to increase drag to more than about one-half the rated line test. More courts disaster. Cranked-up drags lose more game fish than all other errors combined.

Having completed a fishing trip, back the drag all the way off. This is a delicate mechanism and a few days of tight pressure may cause binding just when you least need it. Rings and

*In Argentina, a Traful Lake trophy tests light spinning tackle.
(Photo by Erwin A. Bauer)*

washers may have to be replaced from time to time, and you
may want to think about Teflon washers, which are installed
in some of the better reels but have to be added to the mediocre types.

Nothing is all-purpose and each tackle combination has its
limitations. Each is supreme in one little sphere of absolute
efficiency, and this is true of spinning. It was designed, and it
is, a light-casting nonpareil. If you go overly heavy, then the

combination is out of its class. Those who insist on throwing flies with bubble floats or sinkers are equally wrong. Revolving-spool works better in trolling, so what do you prove by working with ill-chosen tools?

In trout fishing, the word is ultralight. With miniature lures or baits, the angler can phase down to 4- or even 2-pound-test strands of fine monofilament, so long as the rod is balanced to this gossamer thread. You'll need a very limber tip and a smooth reel drag. Modern spinning reels are good, and they'll be better as manufacturers compete.

Any casting rod, and I don't care which discipline is involved, boils down to the stick that throws an apple. If that "apple" is light, then you must have a limber and resilient tip. Power can be built in amidships, but carefully—because the light rod demands a light line. A very fine strand will kill a very large fish, providing that it is cushioned by a forgiving tip. The same line would part immediately if employed on a stiff shaft.

Tackle must be balanced, in spinning as in fly casting or in other combinations. It is self-defeating to undergun or overgun, yet too many spincasters try to copper their bets by going to ultraheavy lines. It won't work, because you can't cast properly, you get no distance or accuracy, and the rod is not capable of absorbing the stresses of a hank of string too rough for its guts. A well-balanced rig is bad news for game fish, while any strange combination of the tough and the gentle ensures quick release through breakage. Properly employed, fixed-spool is one of the deadliest trout-fishing methods ever invented. Fouled-up by dreamers who insist on destroying balance, it is a magnificent fish-conservation machine.

On a small stream in central New Hampshire, Tap Tapply and I paddled silently down through a dreaming June countryside—batting mosquitoes and casting to small brook trout in beaver-dammed pools and backwaters. Although Tap, long-time writer of "Tap's Tips" in *Field & Stream*, is a consummate flycaster, on this occasion he was armed with a 6-foot ultralight spinning rod, a tiny reel, 2-pound test monofilament line, and a midget Panther Martin lure. I stuck with the fly rod, and got my ears pinned back.

Tap is accurate with any tackle. He was able to drop that little lure in every hidey-hole and start it back before it was accosted by a savage little squaretail. He needed only a flip of the wrist, while I had to worry about clutching foliage on a back cast prior to presentation. We caught and released a lot of brookies, but Tapply beat me three to one. I don't think he's that much better an angler. He simply used the most practical tackle.

I fished another northeastern stream while it was in spring spate, stubbornly clinging to my fly rod while Jerry Kissell, a kid I watched crawl out of diapers and become a fine angler and outdoor writer as he matured, made me look like an abject amateur.

Jerry, like Tap, was using ultralight spinning—a willow-switch rod and a reel weighing no more than a couple of silver dollars. I made like a Theodore Gordon club member with 5× leader tippets and flies, but *he* caught all of the fish on 2-pound test mono and pickled salmon eggs fed into the flow. Every time he released one he asked how I liked the trip so far!

Maybe I should hate his guts, but I don't—because he was right. It wasn't a time for flies and I was a dolt to let status ruin a glorious morning. We didn't want dead fish, we wanted action and fun. I caught three, and he netted a dozen. All were turned back hale and hearty.

The light spinning rig is deadly under such conditions, when waters are just a mite high and roily, where a salmon egg or some other bait is the crème de la crème, or where you have to reach and place a cast at maximum range—right in a spot that proclaims itself a mother lode. It is a delight in close quarters, too, where fly casting is difficult.

On big rivers or lakes and ponds that harbor trout, light spinning ensures greater coverage of fishable waters. There you will usually employ one of the many fine little metal or hard plastic lures now offered in profusion by manufacturers. They should be small and light, otherwise you defeat the tremendous advantage of spinning and would be better off using a light bait-casting combination. True spinning is light tackle: negate this and you get into all sorts of trouble.

You can troll with a spinning rod. There's nothing world shaking about this, since it merely entails dragging a fly, a metal lure, or a bait behind a boat. It works, but it doesn't work as well as trolling with a single-action fly reel or another revolving-spool type. In trolling, there are times when you want wire lines or weights and must go deep. That's outside the bailiwick of the spinning rig, so forget it. Surface trolling? Yes. In the depths, no!

Sure, you can attach a keeled sinker ahead of a fly or a wobbling lure and take it down a few feet. This works in the early spring and late fall when trout or landlocked salmon are feeding close to the surface; it is disastrous in midsummer, after salmonids have descended into the depths.

In surface trolling, although a revolving-spool combination would work better, a fixed-spool outfit is no major handicap. I have taken a lot of trout and landlocked salmon on 4-pound-test mono and either a fly or a lure.

Bottom fishing with spinning gear is possible and sometimes efficient. First, of course, you have the matter of the bail, which must be clicked into position or left open. If open, then every ripple or gust of wind will whip off line. If closed, then you chance a strike that will be rejected because of pressure. Specialists back off the drag to almost nothing, but this is a poor substitute for the smooth ratchet click of revolving-spool. It may be best to hand-hold, with a bail disengaged so that line can be fed freely.

In some cases trout are taken right on the bottom with salmon eggs or corn kernels. Here, the fine diameter of gossamer spinning line is a benefit where the angler must be aware of each slight nudge. Usually, such an operation is deep-water work with the boat anchored—not very thrilling, but often productive.

You can cast flies with a spinning outfit. This is far from the delicate operation of a purist, yet it can work. The trick is to use a plastic bubble float 3 or 4 feet ahead of the fly, a pinch-on sinker or one of those strange contradictions called a "floating sinker" to add weight. The method is never very delicate, although there are occasions when it cannot be faulted.

A small group of us used to catch a lot of browns and rainbows out of the shoal waters of a metropolitan lake in midsummer when midday motorboat and water-ski traffic kept every sensible trout in the depths. Our ploy was to wait until an hour after sunset, a time when most of the High Speed Harriets and aquatic Evel Knievels had retired to their highrise cocoons.

As our lake calmed in afterglow, the suspended mud settled and the shoreline was no longer rocked by a surf of boat wakes. Trout then moved into the shallows to feed. We caught them on an assortment of wet and dry flies, although the wet was favored because it required less maintenance. Often miniature popping bugs—the sort designed to catch bluegills—proved highly efficient.

There is a thing that bedazzled daytime mechanics cannot believe: if you don't blind yourself with much flashing of lights, vision can be excellent on all but the darkest of mist-shrouded nights. The rings of feeding fish are easily spotted in the glitter of star-shine.

It has long been common knowledge that trout lose much of their natural wariness at night. Usually, if you spot the widening rings of a surface rise, then it is only necessary to place a fly precisely on that spot—and it will be taken. Pattern or color seem to mean not a thing; they'll grab a wet, a dry, or a streamer, so long as the lure is of a proper size.

90

Spinning, the New Faith

Your problems may boil down to precisely two: wind force, and the difficulty of throwing from a brushy shoreline with anything other than a relatively short-range roll. If the wind happens to be gusting, then it is hard to spot rising fish, and you may find it necessary to probe blindly, hoping to intercept a traveler. With the rare exception of pockets blessed by no clutching foliage aft, standard casts pay off. Things get sticky—and blasphemous—when there is no room for any kind of a back cast and a rising trout stubbornly remains just beyond the best effort of a grunting roll.

Predictably, a local ultralight spinning addict can often catch more fish than everyone else combined. He simply attaches a bubble float ahead of the fly. With a flip of the wrist he can pinpoint targets and he doesn't have to waste valuable time working out line or false-casting. At night, browns and rainbows simply disregard the float, perhaps thinking it a true bubble.

A very light sinker, perhaps a split shot, a pinch-on, or a tiny keeled weight, is most effective with wet or streamer patterns during daylight hours. However, under the noonday sun, be assured that a classic flycaster will do far better with his long rod and delicate presentation. The fixed-spool boy can still succeed with floating artificials and a bubble, but he's handicapped.

Don't make any foolish bets about the use of hardware! Over the years, anglers have endowed the trout with more gray matter than it possesses. Recently stocked hatchery fish are almost abysmally stupid, and the spawn of a true wilderness torrent are just as trusting. In between, you encounter spooky natives or well-educated refugees long out of state rearing pools.

Given ideal water conditions for spinning, which usually means a near spate with the flood just a bit roily and cold, nothing is quite so deadly as ultralight fixed-spool and a selection of the tiny, jeweled lures now offered in profusion. Arti-

ficials range from spinners and spoons through a host of minia-
turized versions of hard plastic plugs and soft rubber tempters.

It is pretty hard to beat various sizes of the famed Eppinger
Dardevl spoon, and there are few finishes better than that
almost stereotyped red with a slash of white painted diago-
nally. Mepps spinners can be deadly, and the Panther Martin,
another spinner type, is highly effective. Hardware can be
the answer.

Instant success does not crown the efforts of duffers. An
advanced spincaster is quite as artful as any champion of the
dry fly and he enjoys the edge of pinpoint accuracy in jungles
that would defeat many a derider of fixed-spool. Where a
baitcaster thumbs lightly to direct a lure, the clever spincaster
feathers spiderweb running line with an index finger. He can
hit a bull's-eye at 20 or 100 feet, and he's in business right
after touchdown. He has an assortment of proven lures, certainly not so many "patterns" as the flycaster, but a vast number of choices.

In a great majority of cases, the American spincaster who
seeks trout should consider 4-pound-test monofilament line
entirely adequate, and will often find 2-pound test far better.
This shocks beginners, but veterans know that 2-pound mono
on a limber tip, streamed off a sophisticated reel drag, is pretty
hard to beat. I am personally in favor of the new, bright fluorescent lines, since you can see and direct them.

Two- and 4-pound test suffice for most of our trout, but it
would be wise to choose 6 at minimum if your target is Arctic
char in the cold lands, or Atlantic salmon overseas where
fixed-spool is allowed. These members of the clan grow to
heroic size and are capable of running off with a lot of string.
Similarly, 6 might be a far wiser test in a cold-water hunt for
big lake trout (togue) when they are feeding on the surface
and in the shallows during spring and late fall.

Monofilament is a synthetic, carefully extruded from petro-
leum products and various catalysts. Some have been conned
into thinking that it is the ultimate, without fault, but that is

Brown and rainbow trout brought to account on a string of flashing spinners and sewed shiner baits.

an error. This strand will see continual improvement, yet it currently reigns absolutely supreme in spinning. There are various conformations, but a spincaster should always insist on round mono; the flat or ribbon type has its uses, but is prone to much twisting. Never use it with fixed-spool.

I have read some wishful thinking to the effect that mono does not absorb water. It does, up to 2 or 3 percent of bulk even when stored in a room of average temperature and humidity, and much more when in use. Moreover, absorption of water lessens the pound-test rating: a line, or leader, immersed for two or three hours drops an average of 10 to 15 percent of its rated pound test when dry. Wet nylon is much more susceptible to fraying than dry, and the stuff stretches.

In fact, it stretches like an elastic band! Most of the modern strands elongate 20 to 33 percent before they pop. This isn't the disaster it seems, particularly in the short-range operation of light spinning tackle where it is even a safety valve. Stretch is not a four-letter word because, kept within bounds, it adds a measure of insurance.

All lines stretch, even single-strand metal. If they didn't, then there would be immediate crystallization and breakage. The industrial trick, with mono, is to ensure controlled stretch, plus knot factor, plus durability. There will be better strands, and pretty soon we'll see one that does not absorb moisture and weaken. It's still the only line for fixed-spool.

Mono is slippery, so knots must be fairly sophisticated. Most of us go with the Improved Clinch, an excellent fastening and one that should be learned at the very outset. There are all sorts of connections and I recommend the study of a book called *Practical Fishing Knots*, by Lefty Kreh and Mark Sosin. Both are recognized authorities and they have researched various fastenings on the fishing grounds.

Sometimes we get overzealous in the promotion of light tackle and the sport ensured thereof. An unschooled angler, especially a beginner, should always go a mite heavier than the ideal clarioned by experts. There's nothing wrong with 6-pound test on small trout; it won't cast as far as lighter extrusions and it may be slightly more visible to the educated fish, yet it does the job well and provides a cushion. Initially, a man wants to catch a fish. Later, it is great fun to specialize, and still catch a fish with the lightest possible practical gear. Learn the basics before progressing to the heights.

6

Knighthood
At Last!

There are trout fishermen who enjoy long and fruitful lives without ever casting a fly, and there are masters who know all of the intricacies—yet prefer to fool a wary customer on artfully presented natural bait. I think a majority of us who are intrigued by delicate angling come around to the fly, not solely because it is most efficient, or because of romance and status, but simply due to the fact that there are conditions when no other technique is quite so deadly.

In my opinion it is rather silly to be a purist for any reason other than a heartfelt desire to fish in that manner. It is impossible to argue with a man who respects each of the approaches, yet shrugs and declares that he prefers dry flies alone, or wets, or whatever. Irritation develops when a self-proclaimed specialist implies that anything other than his chosen method indelibly marks a second-class citizen.

My own fishing for trout during the past few decades (other than in tiny streams) has been almost entirely confined to the use of flies, yet the choice is a handicap if seasonal success must be counted as the number of fishes brought to net and either kept or released. Classic fly-fishing is dependent on water conditions as well as season, weather, and time of day. It is rather futile to defend the art zealously as a do-all when deep trollers, spincasters, and clever baitmen succeed year around. Ideally, one changes weapons and tactics as need becomes apparent.

Those of us who are well hooked may be honest men if we can smile ruefully and say: "Fly casting isn't *always* deadliest, but for me it happens to be the most soul-satisfying way to a trout." There is a tremendous challenge, and there is a delicacy matched only in ultralight baiting in a trickle.

Certainly a great number of anglers feel this challenge and rise to it, yet there are capable performers who joined the club for reasons precisely opposite: they enlisted when convinced that the long wand, at times, could be deadlier than anything in their arsenals. I recall a typical case.

There is a lake in central Massachusetts that is well stocked with brown and rainbow trout. These are all hatchery fish, yet there is considerable carry-over due to a native population of smelt. For a couple of months in spring and fall, surface feeders are abundant and that's when my brothers and I launch a canoe and hunt them with wets, dries, and selected streamer patterns.

A friend who had wedded himself to angling relatively late in life was taking fair catches with deep-trolling tackle. He was on the grounds late one afternoon when my brother Dick and I were boating ten to his one—and releasing all of the fish. They were feeding right on the surface and every cast to a rise seemed to ensure a quick strike. Our deep-trolling buddy made a social call.

He said, "I never used a fly rod in my life, but I want to learn. Will you tell me exactly what to buy, and will you give me some basic instruction?"

We did those little things and within a few weeks he became a pretty good flinger of flies. There was just one sour note: our friend was prone to growl about "all the years I've wasted!"

It's a rather common delusion that fly casting requires consummate skill. A few experts unintentionally foster this nonsense with learned treatises that scare newcomers right out of their boots. The average sportsman may never attain the mastery of a Lee Wulff or a Lefty Kreh, but with adequate tackle and basic instruction he will soon be fishing successfully and enjoying it. There is no black magic involved, nor does one have to be particularly gifted with strength and reflexes.

Adequate tackle is the first basic hurdle. In fly casting, one throws a weight of line, and not a lure. Therefore, a practical fly line must be matched to the rod on which it will be used. Nowadays, most of the major rodmakers specify the line weight that will best complement each of their sticks. It is sensible to buy an initial outfit from a tackle dealer who is capable of offering good advice and who will see that the combination is properly balanced.

Good local instruction can be a marvelous time-saver, else any beginner is likely to develop bad habits in the mechanics of casting. It is always easier and more profitable to learn a step-by-step process right from the outset than to "unlearn" mistakes at a later date. There are many excellent books on fly casting and the good ones explain nuances of technique. But it's still best to ask for instruction from a recognized expert. Every neighborhood boasts a few of them, and practically all are willing to help.

Watching a Lefty Kreh effortlessly throw better than 100 feet of fly line may be demoralizing to the average caster, who can usually grunt out no more than 50 to 60 feet. Again, there is a mite of deception: *it isn't necessary to throw a long line!*

Distance casting is important primarily in practical angling because the man who can get maximum range is able to throw to the effective killing ranges with ease. Other than on a very big river, most trout—and even most Atlantic salmon—are hooked within 50 feet of the rod tip, often closer. Delicacy and accuracy of presentation are more important than getting it away out there. The fact is, some true distance casters are poor anglers—they trick themselves into displaying skill in heaving, while disregarding the vital necessity to present a fly and fish out a cast. A few go to spectacular left and right curves, together with such other tricks as working upstream or down when these are unnecessary. The deadliest approach, where possible, is a short, straight cast with a fly and descending leader perfectly positioned in a moment of time and space.

Distance casting *can* be necessary! However, where this is a factor rods will be built to provide power and lines will be either heavy forward tapers or shooting heads. Striving for the big heave is rather academic when a trout fisherman employs a tiny split-bamboo, fiberglass, or graphite rod calibrated to light lines. Usually, for best results, think short range, accuracy, and delicacy of presentation.

An angler who decides to investigate the delights of fly casting may be confused by the literature. In too many cases he is given to understand that a midge rod and a 14-foot leader tapered down to $5\times$ is pretty essential. This is not true. There is nothing disreputable about starting with a $7\frac{1}{2}$- to 8-foot rod balanced with a size 6 line. A lot of excellent anglers use similar combinations throughout their lives, and taper leader tippets to less than $4\times$ only after a good deal of trial and error.

In every angling discipline, fresh water or salt, a beginner is handicapped by adopting an ultralight outfit pushed by highly superior craftsmen who have done their homework and know how to use fine tools. Learning is a step-by-step process.

It is possible to spend a great deal of money on tackle, yet a cautious approach pays dividends. Otherwise there is a tendency to purchase a host of things that will never be used because they are unsuited to regional needs. Superbly tied

Beavers often dam a stream, build lodges, and create flowages that benefit trout for a few years and then cause waters to warm.

Atlantic salmon flies are unlikely to interest native trout in small streams, nor will the gaudiest of Pacific steelhead patterns fare well as a cosmopolitan class. In a way, all flies are specialized and it takes a few seasons to winnow out the locally important. An artificial should always be evaluated on its track record, never by the fact that it appeals to a human eye. There'll be lots of time to attain sophistication and argue with the experts about matching a hatch. Initially it will be a good thing to hook a few trout and learn elementary tricks of the trade.

Before making any purchases, ask a few of the locals to recommend a dealer who is qualified. Go to that shopkeeper and be utterly frank: tell him that you're a beginner and want to invest in a decent, medium-priced rod, reel, line, leaders, and a basic selection of flies. Well-balanced and practical fiberglass rods are produced by many reputable firms; they retail for surprisingly low figures when compared to the classic split bamboo or the new graphites.

Single-action reels, like the great Pflueger Medalist, are budget priced, too. Don't try to cut corners when buying a line, for this might well be called the heart of the combination. Any fine line is an investment in future satisfaction and should, of course, be matched to a specific rod's action. Listen to and heed the dealer's advice.

First off, it may be prudent to purchase no more than six each of the fly types considered locally effective. A reputable dealer won't con you, since he is vitally interested in customer success. If his patrons wallop a few trout early in the game, they'll be back to refurbish the arsenal and graduate to highly specialized gear.

I recommend launching the assault with wet flies and streamers. Dries are spectacular and, in the hands of an advanced angler, may be easier to use than a subsurface artificial, but the trouble with a floater is that it requires more delicacy in presentation and a peak of angler reflexes at strike. One cannot use a heavy hand here, and there is a tendency to hit them too hard, thus parting a fine leader tippet. With wet flies or streamers, a take may be solid—but a caster usually "pulls on the fish after the fish pulls on him." Excitement can be disastrous.

A beginner should ignore deep-going true nymph patterns; these are toughest of all to fish properly until an angler has learned much about his tackle, technique, and the life style of the prize he seeks. Figure these wonderful little attractors,

*Russell Tinsley admires small trout taken from a beaver pond
in Colorado. (Photo by Russell Tinsley)*

together with the miniature dries and terrestrials, as new worlds to conquer after basics have been mastered and the game has advanced to that point where the outwitting of a wary trout is far more important than a kill.

There are varieties of nymphs and many of them swim or crawl over the bottom. Others operate at midlevels or right in the surface film—and who is to say that these latter types are not simulated by an ordinary wet fly? The standard wet is, at any rate, highly efficient whether it is cast upstream, quartered, or fished entirely downstream. Streamers, on the other hand, are supposed to represent a variety of minnows, although quite a few of them are rough look-alikes of large nymphs. Observe a miniature streamer in the water and you must conclude that it may simulate a variety of natural baits.

Sophisticated match-the-hatch flies often require skill in presentation, so I think it unwise for a beginner to frustrate himself by trying to equal the talents of a Flick or Marinaro during a first season. Better go to the nearly unsinkable bivisibles, the hackle and palmer types; they just may have fooled more trout than any other floating artificial type in the world.

Advanced techniques in fly casting are well explained by a host of authorities, who are highly competent technicians. However, when summer comes and waters are really too warm and low for peak angling—aside from the carefully executed operations of specialists with miniature feather lures and spiderweb leaders—a beginner can hone his skills with plebian bluegills in almost any marginal pond.

This is an admirable way to learn the techniques of hooking a rising fish, since a bluegill is a patsy for any fly, dry or wet, and is bold to the point of stupidity. Where these grand little battlers are abundant, an early morning or late afternoon visit is likely to find them rising constantly. They're obliging, and if there's any problem it lies in a succession of strikes—so that the angler has to spend a lot of time drying and waterproofing a floating artificial.

Frank Woolner prepares to net a fly-hooked New England brown trout. Note willow creel strapped around author's waist. When lined with watercress or fern, the creel is a superb repository for the occasional table-bound trout.

Still, what better way to introduce a child—or an adult—to the joys of fly casting? Of course it isn't trout fishing, but throwing to rising bluegills teaches a need for accuracy and the split-second timing that drives a tiny hook home with a flick of the wrist, not a startled jerk that parts a fine leader tippet. While the circling play is not the rapierlike drive of a salmonid, nor are there spectacular jumps, only a zealot will declare that, ounce for ounce, a healthy bluegill is less muscular than a trout. They pull hard and there is satisfaction in guiding a fine specimen into a waiting net. Some of the world's greatest anglers frankly admit joy in summertime sessions with the ubiquitous bluegill.

There are, of course, many other fishes partial to flies and some of them are the types that our British friends call "coarse." I still recall, with pleasure, an evening when several of us ran into a legion of horned dace rising steadily. They took dry flies like kids eat popcorn and they were surprisingly strong. We fished until the duck hunters' outlaw afterglow and forgot all about trout while those crazy little half-pound dace devoured flies.

Sometimes white perch qualify for the dummy ward by banging at every fly thrown into their midst. Calico bass and yellow perch like feathers, striking dries in the half light of dawn or dusk, but otherwise preferring a small wet or streamer pattern fished deep. Black bass dote on flies of all kinds, and you can tempt pickerel or pike with any of the gaudy streamers—say a king-size Mickey Finn.

Trout remain the ultimate challenge, most sought after, usually most difficult to tempt. Proper flies are important, yet pattern is too often stressed in our literature. Any artificial lure is a key only if it unlocks a specific door. Much more important than strict allegiance to pattern is the necessity to master tackle, to study the water and the fish, to present a reasonably accurate facsimile of natural forage delicately, in the right place, at the right time. Often this takes some doing, but that is where the duffer fails and the expert succeeds.

A trout killer—although the best of them are "killers" only because they hook, land, and release more fish than anyone else cruising a common ground—usually has two big things working for him: he knows how to read the water, and he is cautious. That he understands the nature of a trout is taken for granted from the outset.

This man or woman—and many women are superb anglers—maintains a low silhouette in approach. He, or she, has previously planned that approach so that nothing will be left to chance. A rising fish, particularly if it is a large and wary native on a well-pounded pool, must be stalked. A specialist will guard against alarming waves in wading, minimize bank vibration, and avoid stumbling over streambed rocks. The slant of the sun must be considered and, of course, such things as wind and current flow. Naturally, the angler's clothing will be neutral in color; bright sport shirts are taboo here.

I do not agree that the moon or the sun should always "be ahead of you" when stalking a fish. With the extremely short cast this advice is logical because it defeats shadow, but the idea that a trout is better able to see a predator against sunlight is nonsense. No man or no creature on earth or in the waters of earth can see better when squinting into sun glare.

Working into brilliant light poses handicaps. Polarized glasses are of little use since the entire broken surface film is a sheet of reflection. Moon position matters little, because all moonlight is muted and the trout of our dark hours are trusting beyond belief. We can cast far beyond our shadows now, and we can see better when we come out of the sun. Make it quartering, left or right. Make it right out of the sun, so long as no shadow interferes. Every happy-hour is attended by a few academic anglers who accept dogma without question. Most of them catch more fish in print, as Sparse Grey Hackle said, than in the heat of action.

Streamcraft contributes much to ultimate success, so the angler who can read good water benefits. Old-timers often spend more time studying possible holding positions prior to fishing than they do in the final approach to a trout. From a high bank, with polarized glasses, all of the runs and pools are easily plotted. Boulders strategically placed almost guarantee a good fish maintaining its position in the relatively quiet flow just ahead of that obstruction. Log jams and undercut banks where the current is swift, but not furious, are worth careful study. Trout like overhead cover, which may be any variety of things, or just broken water; they are more likely to cruise the shallow, quiet tails of pools under dim light conditions or at night than in the glare of midday. Other than at night, fish

are harder to tempt in a dead water. Similar conditions exist
in a clean limestone stream, so that ground becomes the stamping area of tremendously versatile fishermen who taper-down
and make genuine match-the-hatch pay its freight.

Every skilled trout fisherman spends a considerable amount
of time learning the lay of the land. It is easy to blunder on
an unfamiliar stream, but if bottom conformation and flow is
well known, then one problem has been solved. It is a rule of
thumb that if a trout has been there yesterday or the day before, then another will hold in the same spot today. Storms
and winter spates, together with grinding ice, can change
pools from year to year, yet changes are easy to detect if an
angler knows his ground. Big rivers are more susceptible to
the annual rearrangement than are smaller waters.

In many areas wilderness trout streams are dammed by
beavers and the result is a fairly extensive dead water piled up
ahead of the dam. Usually trout flourish in such nutrient-rich
miniponds, but only for a few years. After that, accumulation
of silt, algae, and pondweed encourage an escalation of temperature that drives the cold-water species out after springtime matures into early summer.

Prospecting is not confined to streams. Ponds and lakes must
be evaluated by an eager flycaster who focuses an Argus eye
on the mouths of inlets or feeder streams, thoroughfares, sand
bars, and rocky outcrops that provide both food and shelter.
In spring and fall, trout are likely to be concentrated in the
flow, feeding at various levels, but often close to the surface.
Later, after the vernal equinox has surrendered to high summer, it is likely that the fastest action at dawn and dusk will
be found in the immediate vicinity of spring holes.

Flycasters can do worse than to fish a large body of water
during the night hours. After dark, trout will sag into the
shallows, close to shore, and they can be taken on a variety
of wets, dries, and streamers. Color of the fly becomes less
important—the night-roving trout is as likely to grab an all-
black offering as an all-white one. Evidently they spot the

silhouette of the lure against the sky. Night trout fishing often produces trophy catches, for the quarry loses much of its natural wariness between dusk and dawn. The less overhead light, the less chance to see something unnatural, and so to spook.

Fly casting is challenging if only because there are so many variables—all of which can be explained, but rarely *are* explained due to a host of conflicting opinions dating back as far as Walton, Halford, and Skues, updated by America's Gordon, Hewitt, La Branche, and the present authorities. All have much to offer, yet none has said the final word. Trout fishing will progress, even though burdened by outmoded opinion, tradition retained solely because it smacks of romance, and sometimes because a revered elder statesman said it. In no other sport are we so thoroughly ensnared, bound in wraps of faith. Even the new masters get so wrapped up in Latin phraseology that a reasonably intelligent layman can't understand their books on Ephemeridae.

These lofty authorities offer much of importance, yet it is quite possible, in the pursuit of ultraspecialization, to alienate the average angler and to present this delightful game as a sport reserved for erudite professionals who can quote Isaac Walton at length. Actually, fly casting for trout is elementary, easy to learn, pleasant in execution, and very productive without highly sophisticated technique.

Dogma should be a four-letter word. You can fish a fly in many ways, not solely as advocated by piscatorial field marshals. "Dap" it—as Isaac Walton directed. Fish it upstream, downstream, or quarter the current. Feed a tiny feather artificial into a brushy trickle and then bring it back in short darts. While observing the niceties, it is wise to be an opportunist and to take advantage of any unusual situation. Rules, they say, are made to be broken, and rigidly academic anglers catch a minimum of trout.

Ideally, the upstream cast is most effective with a dry fly, and may be as well chosen with a wet or nymph. There are good reasons for this, primarily the advantages of a drag-free

Arnold Laine casting on the Campground Pool of Grand Lake Stream, Maine.

float, plus the fact that trout lie with their heads into the flood and thus observe less aft. Unfortunately, there are places where it is absolutely impossible to throw upcurrent, and then meticulous casting is necessary so that there will be no drag until the fly has passed over a trout's window. Long before Leonard M. Wright, Jr., wrote a delightful book called *Fishing the Dry Fly As a Living Insect*, unlettered countrymen were doing just that by the downstream skittering of floating artificials. At times the technique is highly effective, if only because—as Wright observes—it simulates escaping forage, a living insect.

Some years back, Canadian Atlantic salmon fishermen were shocked by the success of a floating tempter called the Bomber. It is a clipped deer-hair and palmer-hackled artificial that looks more like a bass bug than anything else, and it is often deadly when fished downstream and literally skated across the surface like a miniature outboard motorboat. The fresh-run salmon is supposed to strike at a memory, but wherever did those silvery gladiators see anything like this in nature?

You can work a dry fly up, across the current flow so that it quarters for a brief period prior to dragging, or down, where it begins to riffle and skitter. Lots of trophy trout have been hooked on ill-presented dry flies that got waterlogged and submerged. Purists, strangled by dogma, fear to mention the unusual occurrence to do so would risk drumming out of the Theodore Gordon True Church. Yet there is always a reason for a thing that happens. Perhaps it would be better to seek reasons and—sacrilege—to question the masters in a search for truth.

Traditionally, a wet fly is cast down and across a flow at a nice angle so that it quarters and swings just ahead of a known or suspected trout's holding place. Line is mended, and a strike may be expected at any point, even during the first moments of retrieve after a swing. You may see a quick flash before the line tightens up or, if observant, see the line itself twitch before its belly has been snugged up and the fish is on and running.

Streamer flies are employed in much the same manner, and the miniatures often simulate a wet pattern or a high-riding nymph. Big streamers often fare best on sinking lines when they are swept close to the bottom in a deep pool. It is, almost traditionally, a cross-stream quartering cast accurately placed to ensure that the lure swings through potentially productive territory. A line must be mended almost instinctively, a thing that gets to be natural operating procedure.

Nymphs are another thing. Usually they are cast upstream and fished close to the bottom. There it takes a discerning angler to sense the miniscule bump of a strike and raise his rod tip. Nymphs also take fish on the round-about downstream swing, and one must always remember that some of the naturals ride surface layers. Wet flies and nymphs are closely allied, and some of the most productive wets in the world are really nymphs in disguise. If you choose to delude yourself, do so because it's all in fun.

Traditional methods are best because a host of great anglers have experimented and found this to be so. However, if a thing does not work it is rather stupid to accept failure prior to experimenting. If a fly that apparently matches the hatch produces no strikes, there'll be no thunderclap if you experiment with something radically different. A good fisherman's mind is never locked into senseless tradition. If they're feeding, then they'll take *something*.

To a certain extent fly-fishing can be a year-round sport, or nearly so. An increasing number of northern states now allow angling in open water during the winter months, a game reserved for zealots because it is both cold and dangerous. One treads snow-covered or icy banks, and a slip means inundation in near-freezing water. Nonetheless, fish can be taken, usually on sinking lines, wet flies, streamers, or nymphs fished slowly. There will be no hatches or fast sport, for winter-over trout are logy and feed sporadically. Retrieve must therefore be slowed to an absolute crawl, which may be defeated by current flow. In a pond, where there is no appreciable movement of the water, best winter results are obtained by allowing a fly to sink and then by inching it along the bottom. It can be done, and I have done it, but I do not consider this particular phase of the sport a glorious adventure.

Water temperature and season will determine optimum levels and rates of retrieve where subsurface artificials are employed. Dries, quite naturally, fare best when natural insects are hatching. It is tempting to prepare neat little graphs outlining ideal temperatures for the various salmonids, but I leave this to more academic anglers who ignore the fact that even in a given region there'll be considerable variations. Of the big three, a brook trout feeds most avidly in cold water, while browns and rainbows shrug off higher temperatures. All, of course, are cold-water fishes; when surface layers warm they will head for the depths.

Larger flies and heavier leader tippets are usually feasible when a stream is at normal level or in partial spate. As levels decline, usually during the hot months, one must concentrate on tiny flies and long leaders tapered down to extremely fine tippets. Presentation then becomes even more of an art form and there is little margin for error. Clumsy performance seldom produces results when waters are low, crystal clear, and as warm as they are likely to get.

How long a leader? Advanced anglers make their own, fitting the punishment to the crime as circumstances demand. The norm is probably 9 feet from butt loop to the end of a tippet, yet this is deceptive because most of us nail-knot a 2-foot section of heavy mono to the end of a line, then chop the butt loop off the prepared leader and blood-knot it to the short extension. Therefore the entire trace (as Europeans call it) will be approximately 11 feet.

Avoid butt loops because they are "bubble makers." Ideally, connect the fly line right into the heavy extension, attach the leader to this with a slim little blood knot. There'll be nothing to create commotion or to snag a drifting stem of grass.

Taper can be important, since a well-made leader constructed of a stiffer monofilament than that used for standard spinning aids in turning a light fly over at the end of a cast.

Under normal conditions one need go no lighter than 3× or 4× at tippet, although there are occasions when something much finer is necessary. When that happens, the angler had better be equipped with a forgiving rod, and he had best know how to control his emotions at strike. Good leaders are available at a pittance. They are necessary, even though some trout and salmon can be dunces.

A few years ago a local acquaintance came to me early in September seeking information about fishing locations. I advised him to try a thoroughfare in northern Maine where landlocked salmon congregated annually, in the fall. The fish had always seemed partial to small wet flies, and I named patterns.

A week later this character returned, elated. He had a large cooler full of landlocks ranging from 3 to 6 pounds—enough to have earned a jail sentence if the busy wardens had caught him in possession.

After growling about taking too many, I asked how fine he had to taper down—and he didn't know what I was talking about. When I explained, he said: "Hell, we used 4 or 5 feet of 6-pound-test monofilament!"

Rules, I repeat, are made to be broken, but don't count on scoring as a maverick; this was an exception to prove the rule. I just shook my head and wished I'd been there. Even a broken-down outdoor writer would have scored, but I'd have returned 99 percent of those glorious warriors to the thoroughfare. Fly-fishing should be for fun, not for slaughter.

Don't knock the level leader as a beginner's fault, because some exceptionally knowledgeable Atlantic salmon fishermen now prefer it and even go to the short 6-foot trace. Simply understand that taper is necessary where absolute delicacy of presentation is a must, where the fish are wary and casts are relatively long. Leaders can be tricky things.

The ideal is probably a straight, tapered extrusion with no knots, unless you choose to add a fine tippet to the end. It's good, and yet maybe still utopian because some continue to feel that the extruded taper is trouble prone because of built-

Arnold Laine paddles while Bob Williams nets a heavy square-tail taken on a double-hooked streamer fly and monofilament line.

in air bubbles and other failures. I have never experienced such leader failure, but must admit that most of my extruded tapers have been employed on big fish where the tippet was pretty stout. This conformation has to be the ultimate, and it will be.

Quite naturally, those graduated in taper by means of 18- or 20-inch lengths of monofilament connected with blood knots incorporate a predictable loss of strength. No knot is truly 100 percent, and every knot is a potential weed catcher. A flycaster's leader serves three purposes, all important.

Deep-dredging with wire line took this Sebago Lake brown trout for Bob Williams.

First, it is important to "turn over" a light fly and present it properly. Second, in many cases a tippet must be fine enough to pass through the tiny eye of a miniature hook. Third, it is a deceptive trace that cannot be detected easily by the wary fish. Strength might be cited, but you can get *that* with wire or chain links, and neither works very well in a delicate discipline. In sophisticated trout fishing you will go fine, or you well may go hungry.

There are the usual innovations, still in a sort of exploratory stage, among them the fluorescent strands that are easy to see. A well-traveled angler named Dean Clark came in to distract my work schedule one day, and he said that he'd just returned from Denver where some smart cookies were stringing tiny, Indian "moccasin beads" on their leaders, either tied into blood knots or positioned above them. The idea was that the almost weightless fluorescent beads could be seen and would telegraph a strike on a wet fly or nymph. He said they worked, but lost efficiency after sinking below 6 or 8 inches of water even where the sun was right and the stream was clear.

So then we sat around and made some hopefully space-age leaders that would turn the trick without bowing to any weight problem. It seemed entirely feasible to use sections of fluorescent orange monofilament at the head and the midsection of a normal trace to serve as attractors, as a sort of "bobber." If there are royalties, Dean and I will share! We'll really be happy if people experiment and advance the art.

Armed and accoutred like a knight in shining armor, the fly-fisherman approaches this headiest of angling challenges. In addition to balanced tackle and a selection of basic flies, hip boots are a necessity and waders are infinitely better. After a few tumbles into icy pools where the rocks are shaped like bowling balls and are three times as slippery, you'll probably want waders with felt soles. Some prefer steel hobs.

You'll need a landing net, traditionally a light and small model slung around your neck with an elasticized cord. It will constantly foul in streamside brush as you progress; the cord will stretch, then the net will tear free and come hurtling back. The butt will catch you right between the shoulder blades and it will feel like a direct hit from a field gun!

There are hosts of patented collapsible nets, and most of them tend to collapse at the worst possible time. Gaffs are out of the question on most trout, although they are used on big warriors like steelhead, Atlantic salmon, and char. Tailers have never been accepted, and the basic landing net is favored; it is highly efficient and does not injure the fish. There is nothing much nicer than to stalk, raise, hook, and play a magnificent battler to near exhaustion—and then to give it the gift of life with careful release.

A fishing vest is a necessity and there are hosts of good ones offered by major outfitters. All feature a multitude of pockets for the storage of fly boxes, leaders, mono-clipping devices, scissors, insect repellents, and all of the other little gimmicks deemed essential. Most are fitted with a rubberized or plastic-coated compartment aft, a repository for the occasional fish that will be kept for table fare.

Willow creels are phasing out, possibly due to the modern flycaster's scorn of limit catches and dedication to release. While I agree with the concept of "fish for fun," I am incurably romantic enough to hold a well-fashioned basket efficient, beautiful, and traditional. Nothing preserves a table-bound trout so well as this light latticework, especially when it is lined with dripping watercress or fern.

Creels, for years on end, have been fitted with shoulder harnesses. Use them if you like, but they are unnecessary crutches. It is enough to belt a suitable basket around the waist with a single strap. What matters if, in wading, that woven cage is immersed? Cold water will not harm its contents, and it drains readily.

Hats fashioned for anglers invariably feature a wide band of fleece in which to stick flies. Similarly, vests are equipped with squares of lamb's wool high on the left or right breast. This may be dashing and photogenic, but it is a great way to

116

lose valued artificials, which get clawed off by clutching brush; often, in spite of the wool, they simply "work" in the ever-present wind and fall out. It is far more economical to store flies in aluminum or plastic boxes tucked into a vest. More efficient, too, because it is unnecessary to remove a hat and search through its band, to pull the clinging strands of wool from a miniature hook and then tie the thing on a fine leader tippet. If it's in the box it is both safe and ready for combat.

Fly-fishing for trout is a method, no more. It is an art form, but so are other methods used to seek the same fish. It might well be argued that the purist is a member of a miniscule society, but if he prefers this game above all others, then this is his right. He battles the odds and glories in doing so. The unfortunate result is the fact that flycasters have dominated our literature and have somehow made obscene all other techniques, many of which are quite as ancient, as artful, and as scientific.

Is this discipline, as so many have stated, the highest evolutionary advance of a fisher of fishes? I don't think so. That I prefer to catch a trout on a fly is no argument. As a reporter of outdoor sport, it is my mandate to probe into all of the sciences, not to climb into an ivory tower and close my mind. I am not my brother's keeper.

Fly-fishing already has all the medals of honor. Maybe these are deserving, but we'd better think about it.

7

First Catch
a Fisherman

Rube Wood, Quill Gordon, Dark Montreal, March Brown! Each is a bright and lovely note across the aisles of eternal springtime. For an addict, it is simply excruciating to look at a selection of traditional fly patterns. Each beautifully tied Judas stirs a heavenly mix of recollection, romance, and history. Trout fishermen derive almost as much pleasure in tying flies as in presenting the finished product to a wary prize. Is it possible that angling is three parts anticipation? Certainly there is something almost sinfully delightful in creating a March Brown with the hackle of a ruffed grouse personally conquered in November. Memory is a great part of it as the busy thread circles and a traditional treasure evolves. Every angler should learn to tie at least a few of his own patterns.

Of course it is quite as enjoyable to browse the brilliantly lighted showcases of Dan Bailey's Fly Shop in Livingston, Montana, or L. L. Bean's echoing corridors at Freeport, Maine —to greedily ogle each tray of hackled, feathered gems and always to buy a few of them as an act of love. I hate the thought of visiting Orvis in Manchester, Vermont, because I know it is going to cost money and I know I am going to

Nymphs are still far from accepted "pattern," and some are no more than very sparse wet flies. There are attempted facsimiles of larval aquatic insects, shrimp, mosquito wrigglers, even tiny crayfish. This is the beginning of a new science, possibly a wave of the future in trout fishing.

enjoy spending every hard-earned dollar. There, virgin and handsomely tied they are—hundreds upon hundreds of types, sizes, and patterns. Dries, wets, streamers, nymphs, and curious little terrestrials in companies, battalions, phalanxes, armies! Is there a trout fisherman who can resist?

Each successive season sees new patterns added to the old reliables, and nobody can keep up with proliferation. Good thing, too, because a lot of it is unnecessary.

The manufacturer of any artificial lure, including flies, is inexorably controlled by demand. First, you have to catch a fisherman! Sure, there are stern-visaged masters who ignore popular demand; they create works of art that catch fish first, and don't sell in volume because the public likes to be deluded. That's why a scattering of highly reputable types in obscure shops attain immortality among advanced anglers. Their grand triumphs nearly go beyond perfection. A Preston Jennings masterpiece, because it is just that, is likely to wind up on the wall, under glass, never presented to a trout. Would any sportsman in his right mind ever risk losing an original whipped up by Theodore Gordon?

Flies should be as sparse as possible! A grand old boy christened Alfred Miller writes inspiring fishing literature under the nom de plume of "Sparse Grey Hackle." Undoubtedly he chose that pen name because the basic, lightly dressed Grey Hackle often succeeds where more bushy and flamboyant artificials fail. The late Win Brooks bylined his *Boston American* outdoor column "Dark Montreal," again the choice of a master who had been there under the dripping spruces and succeeded with a rather nondescript little pattern tied slim and trim and deadly.

We observe a rather curious phenomenon. Most of the great flies are spartan offerings. Quite naturally, high-riding and practically unsinkable versions, like the bivisibles, must be reasonably full, yet not the balls of fluff that are favored by many consumers. So far as nymphs, wets, and streamers are concerned, John Herd-Animal thinks himself shortchanged if any pattern lacks a great bush of hackle, plus a handful of feathers and hair. Ask any skillful tyer about this, but only if you have the time to absorb arm-waving abuse of the uneducated multitudes.

Inevitably, there will be the charge that nobody wants to pay for a decent fly, and some expert craftsmen will not work for a sporting-goods shop, unless it happens to be one catering

121

to an elite—that minority whose eyes glow when a perfect artificial is displayed.

It is quite impossible to utilize the finest of hooks and materials, to build solidly and well for pennies. Cheapies are abundant, most of them rattled out somewhere in Asia. The dressing is rather startling colorwise. Windings are neither whip-finished nor half-hitched, and hooks are almost self-destructing. Educated fly-fishermen never wrangle about price; they buy the best, a few at a time if money is tight.

In addition to the big and reputable outfitters, there are thousands of little hole-in-the-wall shops spread across the nation, each operated by an advanced angler and a tyer who is crotchety enough to remain poor because he won't sell trash.

Such a place is likely to be small and cluttered. If there is a chair, it will probably be occupied by a resident bird dog. The proprietor doesn't glide out of soothing, antiseptic shade to preside over fluorescent-lighted display cases; in fact, he may eventually be kind enough to leave his vise and say: "Yeah, what can I do for you?"

If it's hackle, he'll rummage around in a cardboard box and come up with precisely the right article, webby for wet or streamer construction, near miniscule steel springs for dries. In fact, everything he peddles is the best available and, if you quibble about price, that man will peer over his spectacles and suggest that you try "Joe's Cut Rate" on the next block.

The signs are unmistakable; a shirtsleeved proprietor and a few graying aristocrats in tweed coats, quietly discussing trout in the far-away places. Haggling would be totally out of place. The seller still "catches a fisherman," but under these circumstances a sale is bad news for fish as well.

One of my friends used to be a successful tournament fly-caster; he's been a fisherman for more than fifty years and he knows most of the authorities. The man operates a small shop and he is a terrible salesman by today's standards. Fascinated, and keeping my mouth shut, I have watched him deal with transient customers. Until said customer learns the form, this can be a traumatic experience. It goes like this:

First-time customer: "I want a half-dozen Blue Charms, size 6."

Dealer: "Well, where you going to fish?"

Customer: "We're going to the Miramichi, first week in August."

Dealer: "That's the wrong fly! The water will be low and you got to go smaller. You'd do better with a hairwing Green Butt in size 12, maybe smaller."

Customer (beginning to go red in the face): "I don't need advice, I need a half-dozen Blue Charms!"

Dealer: "Sure, I'll sell 'em to you, but I'll bet you ten bucks they're wrong on the Miramichi during the first week in August."

Swallowing his wrath, the applicant shells out a certain amount of cash, pockets his purchase, and stalks out. A few of the smart ones grumpily ask to see a few of those low-water Green Butts and buy, just to be on the safe side. Nobody counts pennies while mounting an attack on Atlantic salmon—or trout, for that matter.

Don't be overly impressed by multitudes of patterns. Many are good and true, proved in the heat of combat over a period of years. The trouble is proliferation and senseless variation. Tackle-shop folk put their kids through school by selling a multitude of different fly patterns, many of which are so close to others as to be practically indistinguishable to the buyer— or the trout. There are just too many patterns and we are departmentalizing an art that needs more attention to proper size, silhouette, basic coloration, and presentation.

Every fisherman experiments, and each feels that his variation is a new departure. I claim no exception, for I have dreamed up my own secret weapons. So now you get a "pattern" that has worked well for one angler. If that sportsman is a celebrity, if he has clout or access to the news media,

123

perhaps his creation will be touted as irresistible. I hold that it isn't pattern at all, until a number of years have passed and a majority of flycasters are convinced. Too often we build a fly the way we build the reputation of a mediocre motion picture star: lay on enough public relations hoopla and people will believe.

Outdoor writers have been guilty of the phony buildup, and I will mention no names both to protect the well-meaning guilty and to ensure against receiving gift packages that tick. However, we've all seen it—the "breakthrough" pushed in one of America's great outdoor magazines. It isn't a breakthrough at all, but if enough people fish with a hairbrush, then a hairbrush will catch fish. So will a beer-can opener fitted with hooks, or an earring jigged in the depths. Drill two holes in a dime and add a hook—you'll catch trout on it, but never so many as on a properly designed lure.

In the beginning it was all a matter of simulating a natural fly, nymph, minnow, or terrestrial. A lot of the patterns are absolutely necessary, but more of them are spin-offs and look-alikes. We currently see the emergence of the ultranaturalist who examines a mayfly or a terrestrial under a microscope, notes that, if a male, its testicles hang to the right or left. This, of course, must be simulated in the finished artificial fly.

Regularly, I have bright young men who arrive to show me nymphs so beautifully fashioned that you expect them to crawl off an open palm. When I ask whether they "swim" in the water, there is an awkward pause. They aren't fishermen, they are fly tyers—and there is a difference.

I have seen few learned treatises on the natural appearance of a curved hook that is a part of any artificial fly, although the upriding types—such as the now popular keel-fly—partially camouflage a barb. There's nothing particularly new in that concept: hooks have been reversed for years, usually in an attempt to make the lure weedless.

If a trout is so delicately programmed that it will be hoaxed by a subtle marriage of feathers, fur, hair, and tinsel, why does

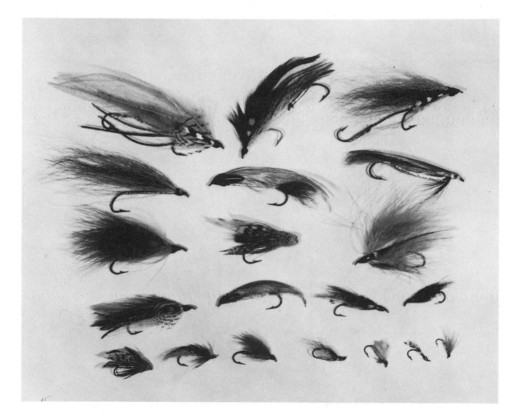

The streamer fly remains pretty much American, although it is used all over the world. They range from the big, tandem-hooked Maine streamer fly, top, on down through hair, feathers, marabou, and piping-bodied creations. Never discount the miniature streamer, bottom row. In many cases it is a deadly trout killer.

125

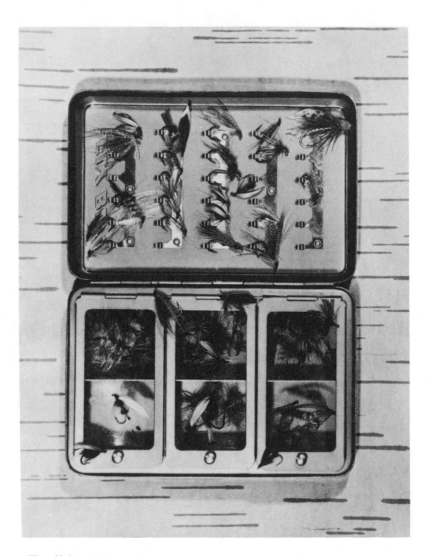

Traditional wet flies may be deadliest of all, yet savants still argue simulation. Do they represent a drowned fly, a nymph, or just something (from a trout's point of view) good to eat? A smart fisherman will carry an assortment in different sizes and colors.

it disregard that absolutely alien hook? It's very simple: a fish is not really very discerning, it strikes a thing that looks, acts, and is colored like something on which it feeds, or it strikes in defense of territory. The secret must be optimum size, color, shape—and presentation.

There is nothing revolutionary in this declaration; indeed I repeat the sentiments of angling greats from Venables to Charles Ritz and Lee Wulff. Theodore Gordon smiled at precise imitation, as did Hewitt. Many of the world's foremost trout-fishing authorities have shrugged their shoulders and stated that they needed only a few patterns, a few types—the basics.

Granted, there are two sharply divergent schools of thought and I intend no scorn for dedicated match-the-hatch boys, although I think they reach a bit. For every occasion where it is necessary to present an exact replica (and I hold this patently impossible) there are dozens of other occasions in which victory will go to type, size, color, and action. No trout has ever won a prize for intelligence, and it could be pointed out that salmonids are pretty low on the evolutionary scale.

We need dries and wets and nymphs and streamers. We need terrestrials and woolly worms. Whether we also require precise pattern will be argued forever. I don't think we do, and yet I am somewhat unsure about it. There are possibly occasions where the *nearly* identical might make a difference. A glimmer of doubt remains.

Many of the dry flies are exceptionally good and should be carried in every vest. Others can be phased out with ease. The bivisible is a fly developed by myopic anglers who wanted to be able to see the confounded thing while it bobbed down through broken water. That's one reason for the whisp of white hackle up front, missing on plebian hackle flies and spiders. The type is as close to all-purpose as anything in the vast family of dries—and quite as deadly.

A man armed with a selection of bivisibles or plain hackle flies in a variety of sizes and basic colors might do far worse.

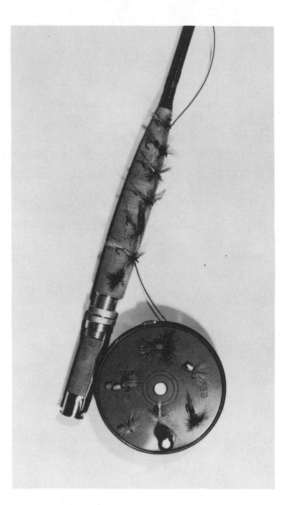

Dry flies and other floaters, such as miniature cork-bodied or deer-hair bugs, intrigue purists. They can be deadly in the hands of a master. They can be a journey into frustration when used by a beginner. The rod is an Orvis #6 graphite, and the reel a Hardy Model perfect. True caviar in the way of equipment, and the tools of specialists.

*Yellowstone's Firehole River plays host to a fly-fisherman.
(Photo by Erwin A. Baucr)*

In a way, he also matches the hatch and does it simply and
cleanly. Properly dressed, the bivisible, the straight hackle fly,
and the spider are buoyant. That all-round dressing may actually simulate the buzzing wings of an insect trying to get off
the water. Woolly worms, much used in the West, less often
in the East, are just palmer-tied long-shank jobs. Fished wet
or dry they catch fish—and that's what it's all about. It is silly
to argue with success.

Brilliant fluorescent lines and leaders startle old crocks, but
so did the advent of the white fly line, initially prepared for

129

tournament casters and outdoor photographers. There were cries that it would spook every trout or salmon out of the country, but no such thing happened. Indeed white may blend into the sky better than anything else, and fluorescent yellow may be even better. We are now progressing to fire-orange fluorescent, both tips and entire lines.

Flies evolve, too, and there will be new patterns. Thing is, they won't evolve overnight and there will be no radical overturning of current knowledge. A few delusions, still fostered, must be scuttled.

What, for the love of God, does a wet fly represent? Some say it is a drowned insect, and maybe it is. Maybe it simulates a minnow at times, or perhaps—I would guess most often—a nymph, since those chewed to shreds surely look more like nymphs than flies.

Nymphs are deadly when well presented. But what's really a nymph? I suppose it is defined as an artificial that goes deep, bumping along over a stony bottom after an upstream cast. You can do this with wet flies, too, and I think many of them really simulate nymphs instead of adult flies drowned in the spates.

But go deep? Come on! There are nymph types that should be worked on or close to the surface, often right in the film. I don't know whether my brother Jack and I invented it, and it isn't "pattern" because the multitudes haven't said so, but we use a mosquito wriggler fly we developed more than thirty-five years ago.

At that time we ran into "traveling trout," bulging the surface, sometimes coming clear as though feeding on adult flies. An occasional catch proved that they were feeding on mosquito wrigglers hanging right in the surface film—a tiny atom of life, but one that could be simulated after a fashion.

Use a small dry-fly hook, say 14 maximum and scaled down to 20. Dressing is simple—nothing but a quill body and a sparse wrap of barred hackle at the head. We clip so that the hackle consists of opposing shafts—very sparse.

*Everybody starts somewhere! A fly tyer of the future isn't
ready to challenge today's masters.*

The object is a tiny artificial that will hang right in the
surface tension, tail down. It looks, hopefully, like a mosquito
wriggler just about to pop its shell and emerge.

You have to "lead" a traveling trout bent on decimating
mosquito larvae. Throw just ahead, and then let the fly lie
motionless, caught in the surface film. If you're accurate, the
fish will scoop it up and you'll be "in." Very fine leader tippets are essential, because this will be deadwater action.

The mosquito wriggler is the perfect example of a highly
specialized fly. There are others, naturally, among them a

131

number of good terrestrials, nymphs, wets, and streamer types. The last three abound in such profusion that only a collector can name them all. A successful fisherman doesn't have to, since a possible minimum of six each of the proven killers usually hits the jackpot. An academic angler may know the name and history of every pattern and nuance of pattern so faithfully catalogued in a host of American and English works, but he won't decimate trout unless he knows how to offer the smorgasbord. Right now we're getting a flood of Australian and New Zealand patterns, maybe good there—and maybe good here—but nothing to raise a fever.

Terrestrials simulate another thing, and they are valuable. However, again I have an awful suspicion that size, color, and general shape, together with presentation, draw solid strikes. You may need something that looks like a grasshopper, an ant, a bee, a butterfly, a caterpillar or—you name it. The famous little Cooper Bug looks like nothing in nature, but it kills!

There is no way to simulate with consummate accuracy, so the need is reasonable simulation coupled with presentation. It's like all of the trick casts, a loop to right or left and so on. Interesting and occasionally useful, but the best cast (with the exception of the dry fly) is a straight line to a target. Throw it in there skillfully and delicately. Plan an attack. Don't rely on subtle tricks; these are for academic anglers who talk big, but don't often come up with trout.

Streamer flies are supposed to represent a minnow of some kind or another, and they are created in a variety of sizes and colors to simulate redfin shiners, smelt, sticklebacks, or whatever you desire. Excellent! But a streamer fly can also simulate a tiny dead fly or a swimming nymph. In many cases it can take the place of a classic wet fly, and do the job better.

Miniature streamers in a variety of colors are deadly. You can work them up or across the flow, or downstream. They can be bumped along the bottom or twitched across the current. We tend to think of the streamer as a large artificial, yet it is stream-worthy when phased down to something like a

A typical selection of terrestrial flies that work on the crystal-clear limestone streams of Pennsylvania. (Photo by Lefty Kreh)

short-shanked size 12. Dressed carefully, it may well be the most murderous subsurface fly in the world.

There aren't many miniature streamers on the market, and you may have to make your own. These may be of hair or hackle. Marabou is excellent, since it comes alive in the water. Traditionally, you use the feathers of an African stork, and this is best. Actually, lots of American "marabou" is the fluff of an ordinary domestic turkey, which is hardly an endangered species.

Junglecock dressing is readily available at black market prices. Whether it's always necessary is a moot point. Most of the traditionalists want it, because it is traditional. Similarly, polar bear hair is in short supply, so it's available and expensive. You can buy anything you want, but do you really need it?

Every sporting-goods shop offers streamer flies with glass eyes, or maybe metal bead heads. They're beautiful to look at and they can be successful for a simple reason that escapes most buyers. A trout probably never sees that glassy eye or notices the lump of lead up front. The lure will be more difficult to cast than a standard fly, but it has one advantage: in retrieve, such an artificial—thanks to weight forward—will pursue an erratic up and down course. It becomes a miniature facsimile of the lead-headed marine jig. What's a fly? Are we somehow excused when we camouflage built-in weight by calling it by another name? I dislike hypocrisy; it's a lure and not a fly.

Matching the hatch is important, but it can be carried to ridiculous extremes. This discipline is relative because match the hatch can be variously defined. Classically, matching the hatch is the exact simulation of a natural insect or nymph in color, size, shape, and action—with a shrug of the shoulders for that certainly unnatural hook protruding. Practically, it boils down to presentation of something reasonably representative of natural fodder.

The folk who espouse an exact imitation—and do so by catching the living insect or nymph, studying it, and building its counterpart with floss and feathers—are superb anglers. They could do as well with less sophisticated offerings, but their zealotry demands specialization. Give them high marks, for they advance the art through success or failure. Occasionally, and only occasionally, they are entirely right. Nobody has solved all of the problems.

Too often that old Law of General Cussedness prevails, and no far-out approach succeeds. Then an imaginative angler must sneer at all dogma and experiment: to do otherwise is both stupid and disastrous. The human brain is supposed to be far superior to that small glob of gray matter lumped in the head of a trout, yet zealots are unwilling to compromise. It must be exactly as they will it, or it is wrong. There is no question, no flexibility, no healthy acceptance of a given situation and a need to change tactics. A tour de force can be futile. Napoleon learned this the hard way, and Hitler went down with a hole in his head.

Say trout are rising and taking a species of mayfly easily identified. You match the hatch with the best in your vest, or even tie a supposedly exact facsimile on the scene—and it still doesn't work. I offer no guarantee, but the solution may be a radical approach, perhaps a huge floater when they are hitting miniatures, or maybe a big streamer. Go to a new attack.

Surprisingly, when trout are rising and scorning a succession of dry flies, they may readily take a nymph, a wet, or a streamer. Some fish are not really doing what they seem to do, so you get into the traveling trout that is scooping up nymphs just before they emerge. A few, particularly browns and rainbows, can be maddeningly unpredictable and a fisherman is then wise to experiment with the two-by-four that "gets a mule's attention." Atlantic salmon buffs get peevish when some beginner coaxes a bright fish with a gaudy fly better suited to kelts, and trout purists repair to the solace of their flasks (for emergency use only) every time an unorthodox clod hooks daintily rising fish on some deep-going monstrosity.

Fly-fishermen as a class are erudite men, yet they often possess a full measure of vanity. Peruse the books and you will find a noble assemblage of tempters named for celebrities. Regard most of these as promotional gimmicks because they are, almost always, variations of existing patterns. I discussed the matter with Colonel Joe Bates, and he agreed, chuckling about the fact that the Colonel Bates streamer was created by the famed Carrie G. Stevens (originator of the classic Grey Ghost) as a fond testimonial to Joe's promotion of fly casting.

Bates said he regarded it just as I regard most of the name-dropper flies, but was pleasantly surprised when a succession of anglers reported it worthy on northeastern trout and land-locked salmon.

Maverick dressings are commonplace, often worth attention. In every fishing area you will happen upon "regional pattern." These are worked up by local aces and, although unknown elsewhere, can be highly effective on natal ground. Sooner or later, if the creations are widely accepted, they become true pattern.

Some famous flies are more decorative than deadly. As example, take the Fanwing Royal Coachman, an artificial that has adorned the covers of more tackle catalogs than any other pattern known to man. Mighty beautiful to look at, the Fanwing doesn't cast well, descending like a berserk helicopter, deftly twisting fine leader tippets. It doesn't represent anything in nature, other than maybe a flying ant, and is really a showpiece.

If I bad-mouth the Fanwing out where pools are stuffed with trout, I applaud it as a production. Breathes there an amateur or professional tyer who does not display examples of the pattern magnificently built on miniature hooks. They aren't for fishing, they're for the deep appreciation of an art form. These classic masterpieces seldom get wet, but they sure curdle the souls of myopic brothers who are butterfingered when whipping up anything more intricate than a murderous March Brown on a size 12 barb.

There are hosts of wet, dry, nymph, and streamer patterns that fall into the same general category—good to look at, but rarely big poison out where trout are rising to naturals that are somewhat muted in color, webby like a bug, and simulated only by a reasonable facsimile. One must remember that much of America's trout-fishing literature was spawned in the East, before our pioneers headed for the Pacific. Daniel Webster was an angler and he sought the eastern brook trout. There weren't any browns or rainbows.

Therefore, in Webster's time and for a lot of years thereafter, gaudy flies succeeded for the very elementary reason that *Salvelinus fontinalis* is the dumbest of all trout. Parmachene Belle is supposed to simulate the brookie's pectoral fin, yet there's little actual resemblance. Excepting sea-run trout, and this also applies to the cutthroat and steelhead of the Pacific, brilliant flies were and are like nothing in nature. Sea-run critters naturally run into bright-colored shrimps, crustaceans, and other gaudy goodies.

Now that I have lost all friends who believe in miracles, together with those dedicated to precise pattern, I hope the rest of you will bear with me for a personal hypothesis.

It is initially difficult to diagnose a trout's vision. Perhaps, as some scientists say, they see as through a yellow lens. Nobody, other than the occasional dolt, insists that they are color blind or monochromatic. So a trout sees the various hues, albeit subtly altered by refraction and, possibly, by that yellow tint. Barring a recent refugee from a state hatchery, it seems reasonable to assume that a wild fish will be turned on by a logical simulation of natural foodstuffs, not by something strange and exotic.

White, yellow, green, blue, silver, and a host of shades ranging from straw through beige, brown, dark red, gray, and black reflect nature's shades. There may be, in addition, miniscule edgings of brilliant red or orange, plus some fluorescence. Rarely is there anything that glows like a neon light as it swims the dark and watery aisles. Where this occurs, it can be a danger signal.

There are, in nature, warning colors. You see this in the common monarch butterfly which, once tasted by a bird, will never be taken by that same bird again. The viceroy butterfly, which happens to be a mighty tasty morsel, has somehow copied the monarch's basic coloration as an escape mechanism.

Almost all of the more successful trout flies simulate the size, shape, and camouflage of a natural tidbit. The highly successful Muddler, when examined with an open mind, is no more than an extension of the March Brown wet and it undoubtedly simulates a number of large, free-swimming nymphs. There are effective flies that closely resemble the natural insects and others that look like smelts, sticklebacks, shiners, crustaceans, or other natural forage.

A brilliantly colored fly will be taken, often eagerly, by small or uneducated fish or by those fish just out of a hatchery and possibly starving to death because they don't recognize or know how to catch natural foodstuffs. Larger and wiser specimens, perhaps those that have been fooled in youth but managed to escape, will instinctively avoid the brilliant warning colors.

The best fly will be one that closely resembles a creature that trout consider good to eat. A human gourmet would probably lose his appetite if a rare filet mignon appeared green. If we seek to deceive the fishes, we had better assume that they also hesitate before partaking of a questionable meal. Of course, we can always settle for the unschooled tiddlers and the ravenous hatchery stock.

Lee Wulff goes to silhouette against the sky, rather than color in a floater. Away back in the dim ages of angling literature, Venables said a wet pattern is not necessarily a simulation of a drowned insect, but may represent a great number of things, from fly to nymph to shrimp to minnow.

138

Pattern has its rightful place, but it is a fooler. Bookmen adore a vast list of English flies, all or most of them nonsense because they simulate nothing in American waters, or—if they do so—simply because they are reasonably close. In this country, each year sees a new hatch of artificials, most of them unnecessary aside from the business of catching a fisherman instead of a fish. Variation is endless, a latter-day copying of Gordon's minor alterations. They can be mavericks like the Bomber that catches Atlantic salmon although no such thing ever lived in Salar's natal rivers. The Wulff patterns are heavily dressed, usually a handicap, but in this case a worthy departure.

Any denial of progress is instant evidence of stupidity, yet a logical man cannot afford to leap upon each passing bandwagon and shout: this is it! We are currently floundering in a snowstorm of synthetic dressings such as dyed fluorescent yarns, hair, feathers, and other neon-bright materials. Mylar, both strip and tubing, has been extolled as a new miracle-worker in fly construction. Hard and soft plastic materials are much in vogue and they can be used to build artificials so natural in appearance that one almost expects them to swim or to fly. They are works of art, yet not necessarily effective out where the trout are rising.

The truth is that none of these synthetics has proven remarkably effective in trout fishing. It is a curious fact that so few of our space age's exact simulations work very well. Perhaps this is because creators have fallen into a predictable trap; they have stressed precise imitation, but have neglected the most important requirement of all—natural action in the water. If it doesn't float or swim like the real thing, then it is a total loss.

Among the new materials, fluorescent and synthetic strands have shown most promise, so long as they are used sparingly. Mylar, employed in minimum quantities to add glitter, is effective. The hard and soft plastics remain in abeyance. I think it inevitable that eventually they will be fully incorporated into the world of the fly tyer, but not yet—not until academic anglers see whether theory has the strength to topple tradition. Few trout are hooked with slide rules, and the true killer, even though eager to experiment with new departures, usually relies on proven weapons.

Lots of "inventions" are throwbacks, initially discarded because they simply did not work. In some cases, thanks to new materials, there is promise of progress.

I once helped to produce a weekly TV show dealing with the outdoors in general. A friend came in to push the then "new" no-hackle dry fly. Before the cameras zeroed in, I drew a glass of water and dumped one of the tiniest of those miraculous things in. It sank like a rock.

He protested, declaring that I hadn't used dressing, and then demonstrated that the larger versions would indeed float after a fashion—not as well as a traditional hackle fly, but they'd float. Any of my ancient dries would have tiptoed on the surface film.

Annually there are great revelations, usually updates of old ideas. Magazine articles and best-selling books clarion innovations, all of which are duly test-piloted by hooded-eyed old pros who raise most of the fish. These centurians then go back to their fly vises and continue to build the traditional patterns that are made of well-tempered steel, natural hair, hackle, fur, and plebian tinsel.

The artificial fly, in whatever configuration, is a marvelous tempter and one that goes back into antiquity. No doubt it will be improved, yet I currently see no great leap forward. We made the last major advance when snelled flies were discarded. We retrogressed with a whole series of "celebrity flies," generally good for nothing other than the promotion of questionable heroes, and it didn't help when a few academic outdoor writers "discovered" things that were recorded ages back. A gaggle of today's authorities continues to invent bits of business thoroughly covered by Isaac Walton when he wasn't catching carp or ogling milkmaids.

But that's all right, because much of the stuff Walton presented was stolen from his predecessors. Study the literature and see for yourself.

There are lots of good and true patterns. There are also lots of look-alikes, minor variations, and impossible new departures. There are outright rip-offs created to build images, and there is outrageous nonsense offered by slide-rule engineers who never get their feet wet and wouldn't know a squaretail trout from a yellow perch.

A grand assortment of artificial flies has been created to catch fish. Unfortunately, for every single effective style, type, and pattern, there are a hundred solely constructed to catch fishermen.

8

Line Aft

Sometimes I hate trolling because it can be mighty cold hunched up in the stern sheets of a small boat on spring days that feel more like midwinter, aside from the lack of ice cover. At such times you may have to steer the craft around floes of drift ice, and may find line freezing in the guides.

Later, when a drift of early summer pollen makes a big wilderness lake look like a field of gold, when the sun is hot and the action slow, then it is soporific to rock along—watching the resident ducks or loons, dragging a lure or bait that may or may not interest a trout. Isaac Walton's famous tranquillity is there, in spite of the muted puttering of a little engine perched on the transom.

For human beings cursed by the fighter pilot syndrome, this may be a truly uninspiring way to fish, yet the record proves that it is one of the deadliest of techniques on any pond or big lake, at any season. Moreover, it works in the larger rivers, particularly in the dead waters when extremes of temperature—usually those that drive thermometers to heat stroke —destroy surface casting in shallow runs.

Trolling is an ancient and honorable art, one that ranges from the aboriginal dragging of a baited line astern to some pretty sophisticated techniques. Like all of the other disciplines, "dragging" can be as simple or as scientific as an angler desires. There should be no necessity to pound home a fact: the highly educated and practically equipped craftsman will always boat more trophies than his lackadaisical colleague who trusts in luck. There is no luck factor in successful sportfishing, since skill is paramount.

Some years before Pearl Harbor, my brother Jack and I used a cranky old roll-bottom canvas canoe to troll for trout. We didn't know a lot about tactics, but it seemed sufficient to stream a complete floating fly line tipped by a 9-foot leader and a small wet fly or streamer pattern. We caught a lot of fish, if only because we were young, tough athletes and paddling was no chore. The canoe waited faithfully for us through the war years, but we never used it again in trolling. At war's end, the big thing was a fast aluminum planing boat fitted with an outboard motor just powerful enough to assure maximum speed and still tick over at a slow trolling pace.

A quiet canoe paddle may be the best propulsion for trout fishermen in small water. Never believe that outboard motors do not spook fish, because they do. Moreover, paddle pace is precisely right unless you battle a head wind, in which case the motor is better. Proper speed is essential in trolling; it isn't constant, it varies.

Unfortunately, we aren't likely to see much more trolling aided by the ash breeze. It's too easy to crank up a small motor, and a guide doesn't have to rupture a gut for his sports just because that happens to be the best way to catch fish. Be assured that I know where power boats will outfish the ancient Indian canoe three to one. We haven't dumped the ultimate at all: we have lost a simple delight and gained some new edges. Let's face it, we're lazy opportunists.

For trout, and I think we ought to include landlocked salmon, depth is tremendously important. The late John Greene, a grand old boy who built the Mooselook Wobbler into a north-eastern institution, used to call it "finding the strike zone." This could be right on the surface, at some intermediate level, or right on bottom. There are two basic ways to go, either soft line or metal, and then there are hosts of variations tailored to needs. There are natural baits and artificials, plus combinations. All work well when the time is right and, as an ancient mariner might say, "when the moon is quarterin' as she ought."

It is possible to troll with almost any tackle combination, short of some ridiculous big-game outfit that not only overpowers a trout but also adversely affects the action of a dragged tempter. Some backwoods types still prefer a hand line worked by a metronomelike arm beat. Bait casting, spinning, and fly rods all do the trick, but only the fly rod is really efficient—and it can be bettered.

A bait-casting rod is too short and stubby for efficiency. Spinning is an improvement, although most of the light rods are too short and the coffee grinder reel is never as satisfactory as single action or multiplying revolving spool for this work. You can't use wire line with a spinning rig, and wire is often a necessity.

A long, soft fly rod—something formerly referred to as "bass action," and maybe now best referred to as a Number 8 or 9—is pretty effective. Snake guides wear out too fast, yet the conformation of the stick dictates a single-action fly reel, which just happens to be a good choice for all-round trolling, whether with soft line or metal. If you go single action, then Pflueger's inspired Medalist has probably caught more trout than all other winches combined, and it is budget-priced. There is little variation in the event that a multiplying revolving spool reel is deemed most efficient. Many good ones are available.

Today's sharpies build specialized trolling rods. The blanks are tubular fiberglass measuring about 8½ to 9 feet from butt to tiptop, sticks that would ordinarily be used by a saltwater flycaster or an Atlantic salmon fisherman on a big river—maybe one calibrated to a Number 9 or 10 line.

Guide placement depends on the type of reel used. If, as many of the finest trout trollers desire, you want to use a single-action reel like the Medalist, then light Carbaloy ring guides will be mounted on the underside of the stick. They'll take lots of punishment, including the attrition of stainless steel wire line.

In the event, as other specialists insist, a multiplying revolving spool winch is favored, then guides of the same type will be positioned on top of the rod, and there will be some changes in grips and reel seats.

You wind up with a highly functional, long, limber rod fitted with the correct Carbaloy guides. The stick has to be long, because you will want to position a brace of them in holders, one to right and one to left, so that they will assure spread. The limber rod, of course, is forgiving; once hooked up, it provides the elasticity to protect light leaders and finally defeat heavy fish.

A former Connecticut Yankee named Jim Rizzuto, a fine outdoor writer and a school teacher who now lives in Hawaii, needled me unmercifully when he heard that I planned to write about trout. Jim counts me a saltwater buff and he is personally geared to huge blue marlin, wahoo, and the Sandwich Islands dolphin quaintly referred to as a mahimahi, so his reaction was to jeer: "I'll look forward to your chapter on millpond outriggers!"

Truth may be spoken in jest. Actually, the long rods stuck in holders port and starboard serve the same purpose as marine outriggers: they spread baits or lures, get them just outside the wake, and prevent line tangles. Fishing techniques are similar on fresh and salt water: it's all a matter of scaling tackle up or down, depending on conditions and the quarry. A half-ton pelagic blue marlin succumbs to the same little tricks that seduce a half-pound trout. The sole difference lies in tackle and choice of bait or lure.

There are all sorts of rodholders on the market and the best are quick-release types designed to be clamped on a small boat's gunwale. You can get away with a simple screwdriver shoved into an oar lock's ferrule. You may lose a few screwdrivers that way, but the rod can be braced against a seat and held stationary. Better invest in a workable holder, one that can be adjusted to a desired rod angle.

Reels for deep and shallow trolling are usually of two types, and there is a wide divergence of opinion. A majority of specialists prefer the single action for all surface dragging, and many feel it equally effective with wire. They have a point, since the large and narrow spool of the single-action fly reel facilitates the laying of line in retrieve. I personally prefer single action for soft lines, but think that a good multiplier with a level-wind worm gear is better for metal. Never think spinning if a metal strand is necessary: fixed spool will work with mono, but never as well as revolving spool. No well-educated troller handicaps himself with the spin-reel.

When waters are cold, in spring and fall, trout are likely to be feeding close to the surface. Landlocked salmon also cruise the upper levels at that time, and there are wonderful spring days when togue are in the shallows or feeding in the upper levels. At that time a troller can go very light and be successful; he doesn't need wire or sinkers, and he can score with either monofilament or a fly line.

In surface trolling, straight monofilament will do, but is never so effective as a fly line. I haven't the foggiest idea why this is so, but experience proves that a level or double-tapered Dacron sinking fly line, tipped by a leader measuring 15 to 20 feet, is most productive. You can use a floating line, yet it is seldom so effective as the sinking article that keeps a fly right under the surface film. A level strand is fine; you don't need a more expensive taper.

Let all of this line back into the wake, plus a couple of feet of backing. This means that you will be fishing about 100 to 120 feet behind the boat. Fly lines of matched sizes follow the course of a fishing craft and are unlikely to get braided on the turns. Problems may be expected when one fly line and one monofilament (or wire) are streamed simultaneously. The mono and the wire, presenting less water resistance, quickly cut across the circle.

Length of a trolled line is rightly arguable. Landlocked salmon will belt a rapidly towed fly and they will hit it right in the wake, say 20 feet beyond the transom, or closer. Rainbow and brown trout rarely do this, and a brookie never. A squaretail will shy away from man-made turbulence. A landlocked salmon, on the other hand, appears to be thrilled by noise and white water.

Contrary to the directions of some purists, you don't need a tapered leader in trolling for the various freshwater salmonids. Usually a hank of 6-pound-test mono is enough, or you can go to 4 if that suits your fancy. Six is enough to land a majority of pond or lake trout, providing that the angler is no charger and assuming that his tackle is right. A tight drag here, as elsewhere in sportfishing, destroys potential heroes.

Straight monofilament can be effective on the surface, although I think never so good as the sinking fly line. Often it is necessary to position a light, keeled sinker some 4 to 6 feet ahead of the lure, particularly if it happens to be a wobbling spoon that might otherwise tend to surfboard. One must experiment, and there are no absolutes.

Back in Maine's Fish River chain I had a day when landlocked salmon were belting tandem-hooked streamer flies trolled on one sinking fly line and one spinning outfit loaded with 4-pound-test mono. They were good fish, ranging from 3 to 5 pounds, and I released so many that experimentation seemed in order.

Bending a Mooselook Wobbler to the end of that 4-pound test, and adding a quarter-ounce keeled sinker to keep the lure from surfacing at the rapid salmon-trolling speed, I caught . . . precisely nothing! This artificial couldn't have been traveling more than a foot or 18 inches deep, and it is a proven lure.

Henry Whiting, a Massachusetts wire line troller, with a New Hampshire lake trout that grabbed a Mooselook Wobbler.

Next, I used one of the streamer flies that had served so well without any weight, but landlocks wouldn't touch it. A return to flies and elimination of all sinkers immediately scored. That day they wanted a surface film presentation, or a tempter working just under the mild chop and occasionally skipping free. But don't knock the light keeled sinker in near-surface trolling with soft lines—often it is one key to the kingdom.

The delights of spring and early summer surface trolling, plus another short period in the fall when waters cool, are transient. At these times you can use light tackle and soft lines, together with a variety of streamer flies. Each area has its favored patterns, and it is time to experiment only when the local killers appear to lack clout.

The Northeast's famous tandem-hooked streamer fly has just two things going for it, and neither of these is pattern. You simply do not need a pair of barbs, one behind the other, so far as hooking and holding are concerned. Such an arrangement may well defeat its own purpose when a fish can use one embedded hook to lever the other out of tissue. A single barb is far superior after hook up.

Relatively speaking, a tandem-hooked streamer fly casts like a bag of worms, and it won't hold its victim in the same league with a straight single. But the conformation lends itself to delicate length without attendant bulk. Both fore and aft hooks are dressed, so that you can simulate a 6-inch smelt or other large freshwater baitfish. Obviously, one tries to size a fly to the forage in demand, and the extra hardware adds a miniscule smidgon of weight, a plus when you desire to troll just below a surface film.

Single-hooked flies cast better, and troll better—if size of the offering is complementary to the single barb. It can be, although the smaller offering may prove most effective. Granting that the big streamer often succeeds, specialists rack up brag-worthy catches with everything from a miniature tied on a Number 10 short-shank hook, on up the scale. There is room for each and every one of them.

I try to avoid any pontificating about pattern. I know all of them and I have used most. An angler can find color plates, plus precise tying instructions, in a host of good books. My feeling is that type, size, and general coloration is most important, not a subtle marriage of hair and feathers. Nonetheless, certain patterns have proved themselves on specific grounds, so it is wise to ride with the winners until you can dream up something better.

Back when all of the world was young and all of the grass was green, my brother Jack created a pattern he called the "Jaxblitz." It caught a lot of trout and, years after he quit commercial fly tying and became a public-relations huckster for the Massachusetts Department of Natural Resources, old customers kept begging him to "whip up another dozen of those killers."

Initially, it was a spin-off of the Black Ghost: body, half yellow floss up front, and black aft, with silver rib; tail, a few strands of golden pheasant crest; throat, yellow hackle; wing, sparse white marabou, then a topping of shorter yellow marabou, and finally a touch of blue marabou. Jungle cock eyes were added—an addition that classicists still insist upon, even if they have to visit black-market outlets.

Jaxblitz caught a herd of trout, but it's just another predominantly white streamer fly. I have a sneaking suspicion, and I'm sure my brother will agree now that the years have slid by, that a properly sized Black Ghost or Royal Coachman would do as well. The big difference is angler conviction. If a sportsman feels that his lure is right, then he'll fish it more often and present it well.

In trolling, proper speed is essential. The pace of a canoe, paddled by a robust man without the handicap of a head wind, is excellent for most of the trout clan. You need to move at approximately 5 to 6 miles per hour, and often more where landlocked salmon are the quarry. We usually troll too slowly for most of the salmonids. When things are slow, step up the tempo. I have hooked landlocked salmon at full bore in a light boat powered by a 10-horsepower motor. That's unusual, but it makes a point.

There are devices on the market, and one that comes to mind is a very simple gimmick called the Trolex that registers boat speed either with or against the current, downwind, or when a gale is slowing forward progress. The objective is to present a fly or a lure at the pace that will make it most attractive. If there is any question, experiment with speed.

Cold-water trout and salmon, during spring and fall, usually work close to the surface and may cruise shoal waters. Therefore, drag the mid-lake bars, the points, and the shorelines. Squaretails may be in so close that a rod tip may foul on bankside rockpiles and brush.

There are hosts of metal lures that are effective in near-surface trolling and can be substituted for flies during spring and fall. Many of them fare as well later, when it is necessary to go deep, but all feature built-in action at specific speeds. A few of the light spoon types tend to surface unless pulled down by wire or a trolling sinker, but others are fine without weight. They can be used on a fly line or mono, and sometimes they are far deadlier than flies. A few of the lures offered for spincasting can be surface-trolled. It pays to experiment.

If such a lure is employed, check its action by dropping it over the side and observing swimming characteristics at various speeds. If the pace is too slow, there will be no seductive wriggling; if too fast, the lure may spin or tend to surface. Angling is a science and no luck is involved. One must present a proper lure at the proper level, and at an ideal speed to interest game fishes.

In surface trolling, simplicity is best. If a fly is tied to the end of a 20-foot leader, use no swivels or other hardware. Dispense with ironmongery wherever this is possible, assured that a well-designed lure won't spin and twist a line. If a very small keeled sinker is necessary, then it will usually be fitted with light swivels and the object is to take the tempter down a foot or so, not to defeat twist. Some additional hardware may be necessary in deep trolling, but even then they'll be held to a minimum by experts on the grounds.

Swivels are misnamed and you will never defeat line twist with them alone—and that applies to the most sophisticated ball-bearing types. If a lure is either intended to spin, or is prone to spin, use a trolling keel well up on the ladder with swivels fore and aft as connections. This does the job well, better than any other stabilizer.

In most cases a fly or lure can be tied directly to the leader with an Improved Clinch knot, possibly the workhorse of all terminal connections. For surface work, stream about 110 to 120 feet of soft line (shortening up for landlocked salmon and lengthening for most of the trout). Throttle down to proper trolling speed and, if the offering is a fly, give it more action by an almost metronomelike jigging of the rod.

Where two rods are used, a single angler may comfortably hand-hold only one. Of course, if our hero is lazy or the pace is slow, both can be racked in holders. It is well to note that any light boat, rocking along in choppy water, will provide a certain amount of automatic lure action.

Usually a combination of sharp hooks, the forward motion of a trolling craft, the weight of line, and the spring of a limber rod eliminates any necessity to strike. You don't have to "hit them," because they're already well hooked by the time an angler's reflexes respond. Actually, too vigorous a strike on a fish that is still exceptionally green and at the peak of its physical power may be the worst possible tactic. If trout could reason, they'd love the gung ho human who tries to snub them up right after contact; that's the way hooks are pulled out of soft tissue and leaders are parted.

A rainbow trout or a landlocked salmon usually jumps immediately after feeling the hook. Browns do this less often, but are capable of occasional acrobatics. Brook trout and togue

Jack Woolner looks on as New Hampshire guide Lyle Prior lifts a catch of eastern (Sunapee) golden trout. These were taken from Tewksbury Pond, where management of the species later failed. Now the golden is found only in a few Maine lakes.

are not jumpers—they swirl mightily and then dive. After a few years of trial and error, a troller can just about call his shots seconds after the strike, identifying his quarry by the way it takes and the way it runs. There are foolers, however.

Sometimes a rainbow or a landlock dogs it like a togue and never surfaces until weary and ready to be netted. Occasionally, a brookie will come clear, and that is something to talk about while splicing the main brace after sunset. I realize that all of the grand old prints show squaretails soaring like flying fish, but they don't really do it often.

It is, however, a very satisfying event to see a silvery trout go clawing into the air a split second before the shock of its strike is telegraphed up the line. Then it is simply nice to be out there, rocking along, half mesmerized by the steady beat of a motor throttled down to trolling speed, squinting one's eyes against the tray of diamonds that is a broken wake, expecting a strike and yet never quite convinced. Everything changes when a fish hits—is on—jumping and running.

Every surface troller is remarkably free of the handicaps that plague other anglers. If his tackle is adequate, then he often fishes under goldfish bowl conditions with no snags or rocky bottom to provide alibis. Such a man can be defeated by a poorly placed hook (not his fault), or he can destroy himself by exerting too much pressure on a still vigorous trophy. Other danger points are successive jumps where metal lures and even the much lighter streamer fly can be dislodged. Finally, inept netting conserves trout.

It is really a simple matter, yet so is the shooting of a deer until buck fever enters the picture. Never doubt that a variety of that ailment is present on great fishing grounds. Anglers get excited and a mite greedy when they see that handsome prize weakly finning alongside after a long and thrilling contest. The tendency is to scoop him up quickly. In this situation, haste leads to accidents and spates of words popular in the underground press.

A cool hand never hurries the operation, nor does he tarry when the time is right. There are commandments. The mouth and mesh of a long-handled landing net should be fully immersed before a weary trout is led into it. Too often forgotten, in the heat of action, is the fact that any current must be faced. If not, then the net's pouch will be reversed by flow and all sorts of nasty things happen. Ideally, a trout, a salmon, or any other game fish is led down-flow into the waiting mouth of a submerged net.

To attempt scooping from aft is mighty poor generalship. Even a tired battler, feeling some alien thing brushing its caudal fin or flank, is quite capable of a final, powerful surge forward or a desperate jump. At that time line is short and pretty well snugged up, so the usual result is a sharp little popping sound that indicates two things busted—the leader and an angler's ego.

I willingly admit to occasional agony when I, or a companion, have botched the job and then watched a perfectly wonderful trophy go weaving unsteadily into the depths. It is traumatic even where, had we boated the prize, it would have been released moments later. Long ago I wrote a magazine article based on the theory that "a lost fish is *always* a lunker." Think about it the next time a companion, crying into his beer, natters away about a lost trout "bigger than anything I ever saw in my life!"

Trolling sometimes is castigated by purists, but it can remain exciting year after year so long as a crotchety old angler can hoist his eely shanks into a boat and go a-dragging. Indeed, that long line aft is a blessing for old campaigners broke in the wars of the big rivers. An ancient purist may grumble about a hell of a way to complete a career, yet his face will light up with the same savage glee as the kid in the next boat when a lovely rainbow bushwhacks a lure and goes bouncing into the air. Finally, a troller is a man for all seasons, providing there is open water.

After the first blossoming of spring, trout may feed on the surface at dawn, dusk, or during the night hours, but they will usually seek the depths after sunrise. Togue, particularly, will be found right on the bottom, as will the true eastern golden trout which is now so scarce as to be almost an endangered species. This is a char, not the nice little iridescent beauty of the West, and it looks like a squaretail with the red pectoral and anal fins of a yellow perch. Those I have caught were never spectacular fighters, since they were small and taken on deep wire line.

However, most of the trout tribe and the landlocked salmon spend a long, hot summer cruising at various levels from, say, 10 feet under the ripples to twice or thrice that figure. You must strive to find the strike zone and, to do this, some sort of deep-dredging tackle is required. There are two popular approaches, plus a new one that will become increasingly favored on big lakes.

First, and beginning to phase out in many areas, there is soft line, usually monofilament, tipped with sufficient weight to bring a lure or bait to a prescribed level. Trolling sinkers may be anything from torpedo-shaped types to the easily installed drilled egg that simply slips over the line and requires no connecting swivels or other hardware unless, as in some disciplines, spoons or lures designed to spin are employed. There, a keel is a necessity, plus swivels as smooth connections.

Soft lines, weighted properly, are best used in probing a relatively shallow lake or pond, since they cannot (without an underwater outrigger, the tool named as a new development) slice down as deep or as fast as metal strands.

Wire and lead-cored lines, unfortunately, are still viewed with some suspicion, usually by well-meaning folk who have never tried them and conjure up visions of steel cables. Actually, a 15- to 20-pound-test Monel or stainless steel single-strand—about average for most trout fishing—doesn't materially hamper the fight of a salmonid. No strike is ever so shockingly registered as that on wire, for the simple reason that this strand incorporates little stretch. Such lines are exceptionally fine in diameter commensurate with pound test; they slice down rapidly, yet there is no concentration of weight to hamper a hooked trophy. Finally, artists who probe the depths use exceptionally long leaders of monofilament, often as much as 50 to 100 feet of the light synthetic, plus a short tippet section of even lighter mono. After the deep-down wire is winched back on a reel, often as much as 200 or

300 feet of it, the trout is played on soft line. They aren't sandbagged.

Those who prefer single-strand wire favor copper, Monel, or stainless steel—not necessarily in that order. I am partial to Monel and stainless, yet both require more angler education than copper because they are springy. If you've never seen a wire line backlash, then you don't know frustration. There is nothing difficult about the business, but it is definitely not akin to the spinning basics you learn after ten minutes of instruction.

Prior to the advent of single-strand, and still much used because it is easier for a beginner to master, there is lead-core. This is precisely what the name implies, a core of soft lead within a braided sleeve of nylon. While easier to control, due to its malleability and limpness, the line is far larger in diameter than wire and thus offers greater water resistance. It is much heavier, yet it goes down slowly by comparison with single-strand of the same test.

Lead-core pleases for reasons other than a relative ease of operation—it is color coded through the dyeing of that nylon sheath. At a glance the angler knows precisely how much he is letting out and can tell a less fortunate friend to go to five colors, or whatever. One frustrating handicap is the tendency of lead-core to mold itself around every bottom snag or rock if the terminal hook is fouled and slack is allowed while backing down in an attempt to free the lure. In this situation, keep the rod tip high and the line tight while backing down.

In deep trolling any given line should be marked at suitable intervals. Lead-core accomplishes this through simple color coding. Single-strand buffs use thin wraps of dental floss, fingernail polish, plastic tape, or beads of solder at each 50-foot length, say one mark at 100 feet, which is a minimum, two at 150, three at 200, and so on. It is possible to get down about 75 feet if enough wire is let out.

The streaming of line is an art in itself and the point at which most of those horrendous bird's nests develop. First there is a reasonably long monofilament leader that presents no difficulty. Feed it out smoothly and steadily against a medium drag or free-spool under an educated thumb. Once a few yards of wire are let out, let the resistance of a trolled lure pull it into the wake under thumb control.

At this point it is common practice among many veterans to push the throttle forward and stream wire at medium to high speed. The first 40 or 50 feet of line are paid out carefully; then, as a helmsman feels the bite of water he can get up on full-bore plane to thumb control a rapidly revolving reel spool. It's a time-saver, but be careful until you have mastered the unforgiving wire.

Kinks in single-strand are to be avoided since they just about ruin a line through crystallization if allowed to snug up tight. Any loop, discovered before it has closed, must be carefully straightened, otherwise the strand will be weakened by more than 50 percent of its rated strength.

Mention should be made of the downrigger, which is sure to become increasingly popular in big-lake trolling where a bait or lure must be presented at a predetermined level and the angler desires to use a soft line unencumbered by sinkers or planers. This technique came out of marine sportfishing and probably scored first notable successes on the Great Lakes where enthusiasts seeking relatively large coho and chinook salmon were able to determine strike zone levels with electronic fish-finders.

Briefly, the downrigger is a stern- or gunwale-mounted device that employs an extremely heavy weight on a stout cord. The cannonball sinker, actually a streamlined type rather than a sphere, is fitted with a release snap to which the angler's soft line is attached. The object is to troll at any desired depth with either monofilament or braid.

When a trout or salmon strikes, the line is snapped out of the release "clothespin" and an angler is then hooked up on light tackle. This is a sophistication of the old West Coast "cannonball and quick-release snap" used by salt-chuck regu-

An aluminum square-stern canoe saves muscle fatigue and permits slow trolling.

lars of California, Oregon, and Washington to troll for coho and chinook. Its handicaps lie solely in expense of current downriggers, plus the necessity to crank a weight to the surface, rerig it, and drop it again to a desired level. There is a saving grace, however; that time-honored western predecessor jettisoned an expensive sphere of soft iron at each strike. The downrigger does not.

Deep trolling can be highly technical. Personally, I prefer flies on the surface, yet I would be a dolt to ignore the tremendous catches made by a fraternity of deep-dredgers: they catch larger trout than the rest of us combined, and they enjoy a longer peak season. When summer heat and drought lower streams and temperatures soar to levels that make surface presentation impossible for anything other than bluegills and black bass on the big lakes, specialists go deep and come up with salmonids that make the purists reach for sedatives. Moreover, I have seen no undue evidence of meat-fishing among this company; they also find more in angling than dead fish and they release far more than they bring back for the gilding of egos. It is high skill and, if you doubt this, try to match the masters. By comparison, those of us who lean toward purism are narrow specialists, not fishermen.

Quite possibly there have been more recent advances in the art of trolling than in the traditional and classic casting of wet and dry flies. Admirers of dredging now employ boats rigged for this task alone and have quickly taken advantage of such latter-day equipment as the transistorized depth-sounder and fish-finder. The depth-sounder is the greatest aid invented since synthetic lines and fiberglass rods. With it, a man can read a lake's bottom and learn more in a single day than he could have learned in a lifetime twenty years back.

You work the rocky bars and channel edges, the drop-offs adjacent to points, the conformations now referred to as "structure" that were once secret places known only to locals who had pinpointed them by long years of trial and error. Now a canny angler can watch the flickering electronic telltale and read his bottom ground as a woodsman reads terrain with a topo map. The secrets of the depths are bared. In a wide and glittering expanse of water, a fisherman knows precisely where a drop-off is positioned. That's where game fish are likely to be concentrated in depths dictated by thermocline, where it is often possible to watch the unemotional instruments and almost count down to a strike.

It is still quite feasible to go without electronics and succeed, a matter of triangulation and knowledge of local hot spots obtained by years of experimentation. Some actually feel that depth-sounders and fish-finders should be outlawed because they are too efficient.

Lures are multitudinous and they change from one area to another. Each is one that has succeeded and is perpetuated. There are old standards that survive because they work, and there are newcomers that cannot be disregarded since they turn the trick with relative ease. It is always a traumatic experience for a local guide when some auslander murders trout with a new lure or method. He hates it, wars against it, and finally adopts it since he cannot afford to do otherwise.

First of the great deep-trolling lures, at least in point of seniority, is the spoon. These metal tempters still catch more trout, salmon, and togue than any other combination of artificials worked close to the bottom, and early birds like the Pflueger Chum Spoon and the Eppinger Dardevl are now augmented by a considerable variety of shapes and slim, deadly variations.

Plugs of many basic types now make inroads on the metal menagerie and the Helin Flatfish was certainly among the first of the legions. It is a deadly little plug and detractors can cite no fault other than a necessity to troll very slowly. If there is a general rule of thumb which declares that anglers usually err in dragging a lure at low speeds, it doesn't apply to the murderous Flatfish.

Several of the so-called "Finnish Minnows" have proved their worth in the depths. Rapala and Rebel are best known, although there are hosts of lookalikes—some good, and some built to catch fishermen instead of fish. It should be emphasized that an angler is always best served if he buys the original of a successful type. Only rarely (although it happens) will a copy-cat version produce as well.

A third great family of trolling lures encompasses revolving spoon spinner-flasher combinations, and these are usually employed with natural bait as a terminal attraction. Never say always, because a string of spoons and flashers can also bring a salmonid up to check a tail-end streamer fly or swimming plug.

The hypothesis is elementary: a string of revolving flashers, such as the well-known Davis Spoon rig, simulates a small school of predators rushing baitfish. The come-hither flash attracts trout or salmon, and there is also the sound of whirling metal, a factor yet to be adequately documented, but which most authorities believe is important.

Initially, and possibly still 90 percent of the time, a Davis Spoon rig or one of many similar designs, is tipped with some fresh sewed-on bait, such as a shiner, a smelt, a chub of proper size, or even a gob of angleworms. There is method in this because fish possess a sense of smell, or call it taste. The natural bait exudes a thin stream of scent-taste that may be irresistible under certain conditions.

Flashers attract salmonids, so they also fare well when the trailing tidbit is a spoon, a plug, or a streamer fly. Catch-22 is the fact that one now deals with a rather bulky and water-resistant "Christmas Tree" in order to hook trout that may be overpowered by the very weight of the rig. Tackle, accordingly, must be beefed up and some joy in the playing of a fish is lost.

Moreover, when using a string of flashers, it is usually necessary to add BB shot, egg sinkers, swivels, and connections, plus a rudder keel to prevent line twist. None of these need be heavy; indeed, plastic keels do as well as the old hammered copper, lead, and aluminum types, but the end result is a conglomeration of swivels, a keel, spinners graduated in size, another snap swivel, a short leader, and a chosen hook on which a bait has been carefully sewed. Or, of course, an artificial lure in lieu of fresh bait. Because a string of flashers revolves rather ponderously, you'll have to accept gear that cannot be called ultralight—and you are certainly going to lose some large fish because they tend to tear off after hook-up.

A few poor souls who have spent more time reading the literature than making history under a wide sky remain convinced that trout and salmon are color blind. They are not, and they can be unpredictable. Chrome, copper, and brass probably lead in spoons and wobblers, yet there are days when nothing will do other than a lure painted in one of the new fluorescent reds or fire-orange, white with red spots, standard orange, or some other hue.

Deep-going plug finishes are quite as important and I will not attempt to offer reasons. However, you will find days when it is profitable to paint a streak of fluorescent red down the side of a Rapala or Rebel accoutred in some standard blue and silver factory dress. There are good reasons for a variety of finishes (aside from the catching of fishermen) that lead reputable firms to offer a wide variety of color schemes.

It works with spoons and flashers, too, possibly due to the slant and amount of light, plus the clarity of water and depth worked, but any doubter will be convinced if he trolls a string of brass spoons to starboard and another rig of chrome to port. Providing that both outfits are equally balanced regarding line, weight, size, and lure—that which draws a majority of strikes *must* have something going for it.

In trolling, particularly, surface work, weather, and wind conditions can be quite as important as they are in any other technique. A flat calm rarely is so promising as a brisk chop, and a breeze from the south often seems to drive bait into a fish's mouth. Weather fronts can trigger fast action, usually just prior and just after changes occur. Most of the salmonids are affected by barometric pressure.

Tap Tapply, like most of us in the Northeast, likes to fish on what he calls "a soft day," with warm cloud cover and gentle wind out of the southwest—always enough to stir a nice "salmon ripple." On any "hard" or "sharp" day, bright and cool with a north or northeast wind, it may be better to weed the garden. However, in planning a trip you cannot always count on ideal weather and water conditions. Nobody catches a fish unless he has a line in the water.

Trolling has been called a lazy man's game, and it can be that. It can also be highly sophisticated, a probing of the surface, the middepth thermoclines, and unseen bottom contours. A complete angler should understand all of the various techniques and use each in its proper place. Each is a royal road to adventure and life is too short to be a zealot.

9

Launch All Boats!

Calendar art and old prints traditionally feature an Indian birchbark canoe with a sportsman perched in the bow and a gallused countryman paddling. The water is glass smooth, stained by a spectacular sunset. Usually the guide has a pipe stuck in his mouth. A brook trout will be leaping in the foreground and there'll be a bull moose standing on a near point.

That's pretty romantic, although a cynic might offer mild rebuttal. Bark canoes are now very scarce, glass-smooth water is a sometime thing, and any big lake can challenge the Atlantic Ocean in a half gale. Brook trout rarely come out in clean leaps.

So that leaves the guide with a pipe in his teeth, together with a trusting bull moose. The paddle? Still used, but any double-ender on a big lake is likely to have a small outboard motor clamped to an outboard rack.

Let's examine the canoe, if only for openers. It is at one and the same time the safest and the most dangerous of all watercraft. Properly handled, today's evolution of the Indian birchbark is a tremendously versatile little vessel. It is light, shallow of draft, ideally suited for river work and the prowling of

Light aluminum planing boats serve well on medium-size wilderness waters and lend themselves to manhandling in areas where there are no hard-pan ramps.

sheltered ponds. Manned by a beginner who has never learned to paddle and trim, let alone pole, the canoe can be cranky. No skilled hand is likely to buy trouble, yet the unschooled amateur gambles if he takes liberties. No canoe is a "climb-aboard-and-go" vessel, so it is wise to absorb a few hours of instruction prior to launching or, at the very least, get acquainted during the warm-weather months when a swamping will dampen hide and pride, but won't introduce a struggle to survive. Cold water makes short work of tough men.

Incidences of error are plentiful. Recently a Labrador guide twisted his paddle left when he should have twisted it right, and his bones (together with those of his "sport") are tucked under the moss of the north country. A young genius went into the Delaware River in a canoe, wearing waders, but no Coast Guard approved vest—and they cremated his remains some weeks later. We all wept, but that didn't help. Canoeing is safe, unless you take chances.

Specialized design ensures greater stability in one canoe than in another. My own boating career began with an ancient roll-bottom Crandell, sans keel. It was a joy to use once occupants had learned its sensitive nature. My brother and I used to stand, bow and stern, while fly casting and we never went overboard other than by design in midsummer.

However, friends who were new to the ash breeze often borrowed that 18-footer, and they invariably got wet. Folk who didn't know the "feel" of canoeing, or lacked the ability to roll with the hull and keep it trimmed, cussed a lot. *Nixie*, aptly named after the unpredictable Rhine water elves, was cedar and canvas. She was a high-strung thoroughbred and she died in the 1938 hurricane that ravaged central Massachusetts.

A few years ago I visited the Old Town Canoe factory in Old Town, Maine. There were five levels of boatbuilding then, and away up on the fifth floor three ancient craftsmen were assembling three majestic cedar and canvas canoes. I had the audacity to ask the firm's president when he would go to aluminum and fiberglass, and he erupted.

"Never! Our canoe is the best in the world, and we'll *never* build those tin and plastic monstrosities!"

Of course they did, within a few short years, and Old Town now produces some of the finest molded fiberglass canoes available, plus a far lesser number of the grand wood and canvas models that still serve as criteria of excellence. Rapidly increasing labor costs and the admitted durability of

169

new breeds may ultimately call·a halt, but it would be premature to suggest any immediate phaseout of the old masterpiece.

That's because no canoe in this world is so esthetically soul-satisfying and so responsive. True, costs escalate; wood and canvas deteriorate swiftly by comparison with glass or aluminum, requires loving maintenance if you don't want to spend every other springtime recanvasing, and porcupines will eat the gunwales and the paddle grips. But the craft is beautiful and, in mint condition, will do things better than current crowd-pleasers.

Fiberglass and aluminum are stern challengers, yet, contrary to general opinion, weight is an arguable factor. You can purchase wood and canvas canoes from Old Town or from several Canadian builders that match poundage or even beat standard aluminum in that department. Another desirable feature is the open gunwale, which facilitates draining, remains buoyant if swamped, and is blessedly silent in operation.

Of the two space-age materials, aluminum is lighter than glass. Neither requires much in the way of maintenance and both are fairly easy to repair in the event of puncture. These craft lack individuality since they are turned out like frankfurters in a packing plant. In river running, the "tin boat" clings to a midchannel boulder, while the old canvas job, and to a lesser extent glass, slides off like grease.

One myth fostered by detractors of aluminum is heat when the sun is high. On the contrary, metal is a good conductor and such a craft is likely to transmit the temperature of the water it runs. They can be downright chilly. Aluminum is noisy, perhaps no major handicap in trout fishing, but an irritant to every traditionalist. Glass is better in this respect, yet synthetic hulls always give me the impression of plastic pots and pans whacked out of a master mold. Regard this as sullen prejudice.

There are all sorts of canoes, configurations ranging from the original double-ender to the wide-beamed cargo job that

Kipling mentioned "the click of shod canoe poles 'round the bend," and you'll still hear them on Canadian salmon rivers.

is a mite harder to paddle. There are various lengths, plus flat, semi-flat and roll-bottom, with or without keels. Sponson-equipped types may be safest, but this adds both weight and bulk. Square sterns are built to take a motor that will range from a tiny kicker on up to a respectable power plant on the oversized cargo models. A transom mount is a good choice for work on lake or pond, while the double-ender with an outrigger engine bracket is preferable in river running. There, a shift of trim can lift skeg and propeller while negotiating skinny water.

171

Length is job-rated. There are one-man, featherweight 8- to 11-footers available, possibly an excellent choice for the lone voyageur who packs in to a little pond in the bush. However, these are highly specialized craft, usually cranky in the hands of anyone other than a skilled latter-day Nessmuk. Extremes in length or weight rarely add overall efficiency and often prove a plague.

A very light 15-foot double-ender can be excellent for work on a small stream, a deadwater, or a marginal pond. There you won't need a motor of any kind, but only paddles, because you're going to be bending the craft around hummocks and brush, manhandling it over beaver dams, and portaging. Excess weight is a curse when the sun is hot and the no-see-ums are biting.

Probably an all-round trout fisherman's canoe would fall into the 17- to 20-foot length bracket, and feature flat bottom and low ends to defeat wind. Such a type will be most efficient on major waterways and lakes since it offers maximum stability and load-carrying capacity, yet is light enough to be portaged. Weight is rarely excessive, but it is true that length adds a surprising overdose of bulk in manhandling. It's far easier to slide a 15-footer on to an automobile's rooftop rack than to maneuver an 18-footer up there.

Work canoes, and these are anglers' companions, seldom feature the exaggerated upswept bow and stern that graced early Indian birchbarks and still appeal to the operators of summer youth camps. Pleasing to the eye, such configuration suffers because it is a wind catcher. Modern design retains the best of the old lines, slightly modified to ensure efficiency.

View-with-alarm folk are fond of declaring that one should never stand in a small craft. That, as every accomplished waterman knows, is nonsense; indeed the setting pole is quite as important as the paddle. Certainly expertise in poling is a skill, but so is any ability that lightens a work load. Standing, a canoeist sees his prospective route from a high angle and can thus maneuver safely. The pole adds thrust and is indispensable when streams are shallow and rapid.

All of the lightweight canoes are car-top rated and easy to handle. On the fishing grounds, granting that occupants are well educated in wielding paddle and pole, no craft offers so great a measure of silent buoyancy and maneuverability. Moreover, the swish of a paddle blade complements birdsong and the chuckle of rapids. Gliding over still, air-clear pools one can almost believe in levitation.

Today's sportsmen are slaves to the internal combustion engine and a host of planing hulls that forgive inept handling. Specialization prospers in an affluent society, so cases can be made for each of the different packages—from aluminum car-top skiffs to big center-console fishing machines.

Cartopper, I'm sure, is a Penn-Yan trade name since that estimable firm built some of the first highly efficient lightweight skiffs, but the term is almost generic today. There are both advantages and disadvantages in roof-top transportation. Obviously, weight must be considered and the hull open with no steering wheels or consoles above the gunwales. Utilizing a properly designed rack, a healthy man should experience no difficulty in levering a 180-pound craft aboard. Beyond that figure, eyes pop and muscles strain. Naturally, the lighter the boat the easier it is to handle.

A 12- to 14-foot aluminum planing skiff can be had within reasonable weight limits. Properly blocked and lashed down, the craft is secure and one may dispense with a trailer—although at a calculated cost in efficiency on many an expedition. The car-top boat possesses an advantage denied heavier vessels that must be trailered.

Some of the best trout waters are semiwilderness ponds reached via unpaved roads and lacking any natural or state-installed hard-pan launching ramps. Manhandling is necessary and anglers learn to bless a relatively lightweight hull that can be carried through clutching brush. An outboard

Where rough water is likely, the center-console sea-skiff is a fine big-lake choice.

motor, topped-off gas cans, and assorted duffel make the trip separately.

A well-made aluminum planing boat is a stable angling platform and can take surprisingly rough water in stride. However, for peak performance it is unwise to overload any 12- to 14-foot model. Overloading is evident in getting up on plane at top speed, or trimming in a nasty chop. Moreover, in a craft of this size, more than two fishermen tend to get in one another's way. Needless to say, overloading can be dangerous.

There is a measure of specialization within broad limits. The famous Arkansas johnboat may be a good choice for low-speed work on sheltered waters, and there are hosts of flat,

174

semiround and slightly vee-bottom planing hulls on the market. A big lake can turn ugly under gale winds, so my own car-top choice has always been a relatively beamy marine type that features a few inches more freeboard than standard inland water models. Starcraft and Mirrocraft offer good designs. My 1961 Aero-Craft, a 14-footer, has been used as a surfboat along the North Atlantic seaboard and for lots of big-lake trout fishing. It has been broached only twice, both accidents occurring while attempting full throttle beach landings in heavy ocean surf.

All modern tin boats are fitted with glass flotation, so they won't sink in the event of swamping. That's fine, but I have seen early aluminum skiffs spin like porpoises when half full of water. They didn't sink, but there are no handles riveted to slippery bottoms. Fortunately, other than foolhardy operation in a marine tide rip, pounding surf, or wilderness river rapids, there is little likelihood of shipping much water or capsizing.

The tin boat, wide open and bereft of creature comforts other than portable back rests and hand-carry gear, is a good choice for a nomad. Nowadays you can install a transistorized depth-sounder, and there are clamp-on compasses that point the way when a fog bank descends. Many of us favor extension operating handles. Once attuned and able to roll with the craft, correcting trim almost instinctively, the extension handle becomes a clumsy cleat as well as a remote control. Standing, you can spot boulders just below the surface, thread channels, pick the right spot to jump log booms. Unless it's extremely rough (and sometimes even then) I prefer to stand and ride the craft by feel and vision. For the same reason, most of today's midship console fishing machines are designed for stand-up operation, your knees taking the shock of pounding over waves.

A few of the smaller fiberglass boats lend themselves to car-top carrying, but a majority are too heavy for comfort and are better transported on a trailer. Many of them are safe and

stable platforms: the little Boston Whaler rides rough seas
like an eider duck and it'll perform on an even keel even when
full of water. This craft, and many others built of a glass
sandwich filled with flotation foam, are tremendous mounts
for trout hunters. Indeed, today's market is flooded with excellent fiberglass and aluminum hulls of all sizes and types.
There was a time when builders seemed obsessed with phony
eye appeal rather than efficiency. Fin-tailed monstrosities then
looked like 1960 Cadillacs without wheels and they were just
about as useless on the water. Chrome, futuristic windshields,
and cockpit clutter proliferated.

This sorry trend is long gone. Granted, the mid-70s still
boast a few unfortunate power boats, but anybody who purchases a hull from a reputable and well-established builder is
almost assured of quality construction and sophisticated design. Never have small boats been so completely sound.

For comfort in big water, larger outboard or inboard-
outboard hulls make a rough day pleasant, and safe. Scoffers
may mutter about destroyer escorts that raise pond levels a
foot when launched, yet it's pretty nice to relax while the
skiff jockeys are bouncing and plunging. Nowadays, most of
the big jobs, say 18 to 20 feet, are predominantly constructed
of fiberglass, aluminum, and traditional wood. A majority are
trailer-borne, although many are based in lakeside marinas.

Obviously, the trailered boat offers benefits—it is a complete package, easily launched and recovered. Everything is
aboard, including tackle, food coolers, electronic aids to navi-
gation, topped-off gas tanks. Properly secured for over-
highway travel, all things germane to an angling expedition
ride in the boat, thus providing more passenger space in a
prime-moving vehicle. Unless backwoods manhandling is necessary, this rig cannot be faulted. If it's a really heavy job,
then a power winch provides push-button launch and recovery; otherwise there's nothing very horrendous about the
manual crank and ratchet.

A rubber raft float trip is both practical and safe. This is the Snake River in Wyoming. (Photo by Lefty Kreh)

Quite naturally, any trailered boat needs hard-pan for launching and recovery. This cancels out back-of-beyond ponds unless they can be reached by connecting thoroughfares from lakes boasting ramps. Fortunately, lots of fine trout water, plus such inland seas as the Great Lakes, are best

177

A somewhat larger power boat becomes casting platform and headquarters on Lake Nahuel Huapi, in Argentina. (Photo by Erwin A. Bauer)

cruised in big, fast, and stable vessels. It is a mistake, sometimes lethal, to venture too far out in any craft that cannot survive a howling line squall.

Regardless of size, a hull dedicated to inland trout fishing should be relatively open with no cabin amidships, no Bimini top or other hampering creature comforts. The center-console type, initially designed for marine work on tropical flats, may

178

be close to ideal. With it, there is uncluttered deck space to facilitate casting or trolling. A radio antenna can be stowed when not in use. A small motor can be mounted beside a larger one for use when puttering along and dragging lures. Built-in waterproof compartments get ancillary gear out of the way.

Angling, whether for trout or other game fishes, becomes progressively sophisticated. Therefore the well-equipped fishing machine has clout in that it offers space and power to mount an electronic depth-sounder, CB radio, a good compass, and proper propulsion systems for whatever is deemed necessary. Add a good speed indicator and quick-release rod holders attached to the gunwales and you come up with a pocket battleship for big-lake campaigning. The end result is comfort and efficiency, marred only by an ache in the wallet. Space-age fishing machines are expensive.

Never, by accident or design, forget the usually required life jackets, buoyant cushions, lighting systems for after-dark operation, and a suitable anchor with at least 100 feet of line. In addition to the primary power plant, oars or a paddle should be stowed in every small boat. Away out in the blue a packet of signal flares, plus an orange smoke bomb, require little space and can be important in an emergency.

There is an unfortunate antipathy among small-boat operators toward the use of Coast Guard approved life jackets, a sort of feeling that it's "chicken" to wear so obvious a preserver. Therefore the trend is to use buoyant seat cushions where state law permits. They're better than nothing, but not much more than that.

A cushion is fine to sit on or to use as a back rest, but it's a hell of a poor life preserver for several good reasons. First, in the event of sudden swamping in a high wind, those slippery pillows tend to go skittering away out of reach. Second, they are clumsy to use, hard to grasp, difficult to position when waves are going for the jugular. An approved jacket need not be donned until weather threatens, but there's no disgrace in "suiting up." Youngsters, and folk who have never learned to swim, should always consider the life jacket an essential part of boating uniform—at all times, in all weather!

Anglers are opportunists, often forced to use whatever equipment is readily available. I have fished from rafts made of pulpwood, bailed leaky wooden rowboats while creaking around the springholes of marginal ponds, and angled with some apprehension from limber war-surplus rubber inflatables. It should be noted that lots of modern inflatables are safe, light, and efficient; they can be packed into remote grounds and are often designed for outboard power.

Nothing can beat the Indian canoe for shallow river running, and no planing boat can challenge it in the downstream rapids with or without power. There are, however, specialized craft made for that task alone; they're not much good for anything else and usually serve tourists who want to boast that they went down such and such a river, just as Lewis and Clark did. The difference is that Lewis and Clark took their lives in their hands with available scows, while today's adventurer is safer than he would be in New York traffic. River-running guides aren't anxious to kill their pilgrims. Bad for business, and all that sort of thing.

Large rubber rafts used to be much used on western rivers and still the right choice for tourist adventure. Where fishing is a primary mission, we now see greater reliance on the dorylike McKenzie conformation in swift water floating, and the aluminum johnboat on quiet stretches. Both are oar-propelled to ensure maneuverability and a decent casting platform. In dead water a trout hunter may, of course, operate with an inner-tube float, using his wadered, flippered feetbones for propulsion. One must evaluate needs and go from there. Nothing is all-purpose. What is precisely right for one will be wrong—even terribly dangerous—for another. Boats for fishermen are the designs best suited for each operation. There isn't much future in playing a watery game of Russian roulette.

Where trout are the quarry, keep it relatively open, seaworthy, geared to do what must be done in the most efficient manner. A tool is just a tool. A boat—any boat—is like an airplane. It is absolutely safe when used wisely, and it is deadly in the hands of a gambler.

10

Custom Built
or Cut Rate?

Traditionally, an ardent trout fisherman is a highly educated type who reads classic literature, drinks the finest bourbon, appreciates gourmet cuisine—and boasts a variety of magnificent split-bamboo rods built by Hardy, Paine, Orvis, Leonard, or handcrafted by some unsung genius. His reels will be jewels of precision machinery, so expensive and so precious that no briar dare scratch on pain of being drummed out of the ecosystem.

Is this sort of thing necessary? Sure it is! Pride of ownership may be vanity in disguise, but it is sacred in all societies. Just as some folk read avidly and others collect books for their escalating value on a going market, efficiency of execution may mean much or little. Our Native Americans liked wampum; an African tribesman collects cattle because this is his idea of wealth. Various savage gentlemen in exotic lands have a penchant for human skulls.

The comparison is unfair for several good reasons. First, superb fishing tackle is more than just a sop to the ego of a sportsman. In most instances classic rods, reels, and flies are worth the price they command. It can even be argued that, because of their excellence, they are more economical over a span of years since initial cost is offset by long service.

I think it is only where such a tool is considered so rare and delightful a status symbol that it is displayed on a velvet cushion, instead of going to war on the big rivers and the brawling little streams, that it becomes somewhat arguable. A fly rod, a reel, or an artificial fly is meant to be used—not exiled. The scars of combat are honorable and I personally reserve greatest respect for the priceless gear that has lost some of its pristineness, yet is carefully maintained and committed to the furnace of sport. If this stuff can't stand joyous competition, then it deserves to be filed away in the Smithsonian wih early Indian artifacts and an old airplane called *The Spirit of St. Louis.*

I'll have to admit, though, that I have a few Preston Jennings flies that will never go to war again. Nick Lyons, in his delightful book, *Fishing Widows*, relates a poignant tale of a grand angler who fished around the bend and left a classic assortment of split-bamboo rods to nonangling relatives—who promptly used the tip sections as fencing foils! No mesmerized addict of trout fishing can read this account without a misting of the eyes, followed by unbridled fury.

Yet much the same thing happens when a tyro with more money than skill invests in a masterpiece before he has learned to handle precision tools. I can throw no stones since, as a teen-ager, I destroyed a wonderful old Hardy through uneducated abuse. It is a sin to collect heirlooms until you have learned how to appreciate them. There will be plenty of time for sophistication later, and our field-grade tackle is excellent.

Up in Manchester, Vermont, angling historian Austin Hogan has assembled a flycaster's museum. He has rods, reels, lines, and flies used by the masters, plus much of the best literature. Austin is a true authority, determined to honor the craft and its great men.

I fully agree, and my Preston Jennings flies will probably wind up in Manchester. They are too precious to go "into the furnace." We can always build facsimiles, but it is rather awe inspiring to look at the original, handcrafted by a master. Museums have their place and the trout fisherman's shrine creates adulation when an observer examines a rod used by La Branche, a Quill Gordon tied by the enigmatic Theodore, or a reel polished by the hand of Hewitt.

It will be many years, if ever, before any complete phase out of the split-bamboo fly rod, yet this may be inevitable for a number of reasons. Like the superb cedar and canvas canoe, this magnificent creation demands a high degree of craftsmanship in assembly, hence costs continue to escalate beyond the budgets of many anglers. The kiss of death for split bamboo is likely to come with a growing realization that fiberglass and the new graphites are far more efficient, even if they lack charisma.

Traditionalists will disagree, and I sorrow with them, but it is now possible to produce a tubular fiberglass rod incorporating any action desired. This stick can be light, tough, and more responsive than the adored bamboo. Classicists offer one undeniable argument in favor of the organic material: in the better grades, a custom rod can be one of a kind, possibly able to do a specific thing better than any mass-produced shaft. For a great many years premium Tonkin cane was unavailable, but a measure of U.S. détente with Communist China has eased that situation.

In rodmaking, such bellwethers of perfection as Orvis long resisted fiberglass, yet now market a variety of beautifully designed synthetic wands. It was either that or lose a share of the market when such young chargers as Phil Clock and Jim Green in California produced the tubular glass Fenwick and began to invade inner sanctums. Leon Martuch, formerly of 3-M Scientific Anglers, also makers of some of the world's finest fly lines, didn't exactly extend the life of split bamboo with his superbly designed fiberglass "System" rods.

While this was happening, a lot of other reputable American firms switched wholly or partially to glass, resulting in a great many sticks that are hard to fault. They have their drawbacks, to be sure—glass-to-glass ferrules diminish weight and better distribute action, but have a tendency to loosen after long casting. Glass deteriorates, just as split bamboo does, yet today's models are exceptionally good; they require little maintenance, are relatively inexpensive, combine light weight, controlled action, and power. Beauty? That's in the eye of the beholder.

Like everything else in this world, fiberglass rods are built in varying degrees of excellence. Many of the reputable firms produce premier sticks and add a series of less expensive models. An educated angler must study the hardware and other fittings; if guides, reel seats, and grips are the best attainable, and if windings are professional, then it is likely that the rod has been built with an eye to quality control and may be considered battleworthy.

Graphite is the latest of the space-age materials to complement rodmaking—very possibly a wave of the future, yet still so new that technical evaluation is difficult. Far from an unknown quantity, the name may be a mite misleading since many of the new graphites use different amounts of that light and stiff fiber, plus some of the well-tested fiberglass and bonding resins. Any buyer who lacks specifics can only trust in the integrity of a builder. Fortunately, the top hands are scrupulously honest.

As of now, graphite remains expensive and prices probably won't decrease. The rods are exciting; they are light, powerful throwers and those I have handled seem to require a slight change in timing. The Number 6 Orvis and Number 9 Fenwick, now in my possession, combine stunning beauty and efficiency. However, I'm pretty sure that I'd be able to catch as many trout with a lovely little Browning tubular fiberglass —suggested retail price less than $30!

Today's market offers a grab bag of excellent reels, foreign and domestic. In single action no great sophistication is required for basic trout work, although it is wise to think ade-

Professional custom shops settle for nothing but the best, and there is no bargaining. Dan Bailey and son John arrange merchandise in their famed shop at Livingston, Montana. Marked trays in foreground contain some of the most popular fly patterns. (Photo by Charles F. Waterman)

quate capacity for backing, plus an optional drag if targets will include steelhead, Atlantic salmon, or Arctic char. A few highly regarded anglers think the adjustable drag is unnecessary in true fly casting. But one should plan adequate backing just in case that prize of a fishing career runs for its life.

Reels are manufactured in a variety of sizes in order to complement and balance different rod and line-weight combinations. You get precisely what you pay for, and it is worth noting that the old Pflueger Medalist, which still sells for a relative pittance, has probably caught more trout than any other American reel in existence. The Medalist is a classic in its own right, widely copied and seldom equaled in its price range.

If time is counted in scant decades, the spinning reel is new in this country. It wasn't until 1946 that fixed-spool arrived to stay, and it has been making converts ever since. As has been suggested in a previous chapter, it is wise to buy the product of an established firm, since that manufacturer will offer service and replacement parts. Spinning reels are far more delicate mechanisms than the rugged single-action or multiple revolving-spool types.

Americans invented the quadruple multiplying reel, first designed to catch black bass, and then for anything with fins. The old Kentucky Meeks were built like fine watches and they are collector's items today, but no ancient Meek is in the same league with today's highly efficient little masterpieces. Most of the better ones now feature free-spool, anti-reverse, and smoothly functioning drag mechanisms. Again, choose those that bear old and respected firm names.

There are numerous custom-made and expensive reels of all types, and I think it hardly necessary to dwell on them here. Perhaps you will want a Seamaster, a Fin-Nor, a Valentine, or one of the many new and beautifully machined masterpieces offered by major outfitters. Hardy's Model Perfect is being made again, and it is a joy. I am not about to throw mine into Boston Harbor with a packet of tea.

Custom Built or Cut Rate?

Foreign imports can be very good, or poor. English fly-casting tackle is exceptionally good, and that's where the United Kingdom excels: they are rather sorry malingerers in gear for other disciplines. The European continent seems far more innovative. France, Germany, and Scandinavia challenge our best both in spinning and in revolving spool. Japan cannot be discounted, since that nation's manufacturers are now stressing clean design and quality control. It wasn't always so.

Immediately after World War II we were plagued by a flood of European and Asiatic imports, a few of which were good and a majority of which constituted sorry junk. One trouble, in those bad old days, was the fact that spare parts were never available, so a broken reel was a complete loss. There was a proliferation of carbon copies of classics filled with lead gears. They were all cheap, so they tempted the unwary. This situation has changed for the better, although there is still a need for caution.

Nowadays a surprising number of American manufacturers farm out tackle-making to colleagues in Europe and Asia. The difference lies in quality control, insisted upon by domestic importers, plus a guarantee that parts are available. A foreign rod or reel may be very good indeed, if it is backed by an American firm. Note also that a few Japanese manufacturers have set up franchises here and have progressed well beyond that ancient "take the money and run" attitude of the late 40s.

You need, as true authorities and tongue-in-cheek guides say, "a lot of string" and, contrary to some popular thought, lines are not created equal. Nylon monofilament and the various types of coated fly lines are most often used in the pursuit of trout. You can buy these anywhere, yet it can be a tiger trap. In fly casting, for example, efficiency is ensured by matching line weight to a specific rod, and it doesn't matter whether you choose the least expensive level, a double-taper, weight-forward, floating, floating with sinking tip, slow-sinking, or fast-sinking. Always go to a marketplace presided over by highly qualified personnel.

Fortunately, there are lots of fine products to choose from. The best are never cheap, yet it remains economical to favor a respected trade name while matching type and weight to a rod and a task. You'll never regret buying the premier grades, including those offered by respected outfitting houses under their own names. In the case of a fly line, always know precisely what you need, or seek the help of a qualified professional. This is not an item to acquire in ignorance at a cut-rate emporium.

Monofilament isn't so critical, except in ultralight tests, yet there is considerable difference between cheap bulk and name-brand extrusions. Price difference is slight, so the better product labeled by a proud manufacturer is an investment; it will be smaller in diameter per pound test, far more stable, and will possess maximum knot strength.

Color is arguable and mono is available in every hue, including blue, yellow, and orange fluorescent. A majority of anglers still prefer the nearly transparent mist, gray, or light green shades. For ultralight spinning and small-stream baiting, as previously mentioned, I favor duPont's fluorescent yellow, yet also heartily endorse extrusions marketed by other firms. All of the quality products are fine, while bulk mono will do in heavier-than-needed tests.

Single-strand monofilament now vies with sinking fly lines in surface trolling for trout, although the latter is best. Purchase one of four others for deep dredging: single-strand wire in stainless steel, Monel, lead-core, or copper. These are available wherever deep trolling is a way of life for anglers.

A beginner is sometimes tempted to buy the cheapest of flies and these are *always* more expensive and frustrating in the long run. A poorly tied fly comes apart and often its hook is inferior. Supposed bargains are just as bad when plebian bait hooks are purchased. This is one of the least expensive items in an angler's kit, yet misguided folk continue to seek something for nothing.

190

Fly selection is simplified if you deal with a shop whose employees are well versed in local usages and can recommend, say, a half-dozen of the various types, sizes, and patterns deemed most effective in a given area. The classics are unlikely to be found in cut-rate outlets, since these people usually deal in fast-moving bargain-priced merchandise.

Trout fishermen require lots of ancillary equipment, such as lightweight hip boots or waders, foul-weather gear, compartmented vests, landing nets, leader snippers and leaders themselves, plus a load of other aids, including elixirs to make a dry fly float or a leader to sink, or to keep biting insects at bay. All are readily available at most outlets, although the level of quality varies, as does price.

Fortunately for American anglers, the "spread" is not very startling. Competition among major manufacturers ensures a plethora of fine gear at reasonable cost. If a superb fishing vest is produced by a firm dedicated to highest quality, you can be sure that it will be copied and presented to the public for less money. This look-alike will not be as well tailored or finished as the premier article and it will not be constructed of so fine a fabric, but it will be highly satisfactory.

Obviously, lightweight customized waders fitted with felt soles or metal hobs will cost a lot more than the ordinary all-rubber field grades stocked by most of the neighborhood's bargain basements. However, no city lacks a few small and specialized sporting-goods shops whose dealers will order the finest for a customer and then, if requested, attach felts or hobnails.

Custom built or cut rate? Here's how it works. If you go into any of the famed outfitting houses or the highly sophisticated little shops operated by master anglers who subscribe to excellence, then you are likely to pay top dollar—but you will also get your money's worth. These folk deal in the best and they scorn second-rate equipment. Their "salespersons" understand tackle: they are low-key, never lapel grabbers,

A customer examines deep-trolling spinners at cut-rate "Spag's" in Shrewsbury, Massachusetts, one of a growing number of such competitive outlets where a browsing angler can find genuine bargains (if he knows what he wants) and where satisfaction or money back is guaranteed.

and often seem to insinuate that they don't care whether you buy or not. Many will argue, very politely, about a lure or tackle combination considered unsuitable for a given task. A customer will pay going rates with no discount, unless there happens to be an overstock of some item that hasn't moved and is therefore marked down. Even then, the markdown may be miniscule compared to that of a cut-rate shop.

Mail-order houses range from the highly dependable to misleading. There are maybe a dozen dedicated houses that issue catalogs listing the finest tackle and gear ever produced. They are reliable and, like the small walk-in professional shop, rarely cut prices. However, quality is emphasized and service assured.

L. L. Bean in Maine was probably first of the mail-order kings to insist upon absolute honesty in dealing with customers. To this day, if you are not pleased with a purchase or if it doesn't fit, the firm's computers are even swifter than yesterday's 24-hour-a-day salesmen in replacing it or making an adjustment. Orvis, Eddie Bauer, Dan Bailey, and a number of others are equally reliable. I was agreeably surprised when Norm Thompson, primarily a supplier of outdoor clothing, phoned me from Portland, Oregon, to say that my order for a certain black beret had been received, but that they were temporarily out of stock and would I be content with a dark-blue one. The beret was not expensive, so a share of profit went into that call. The firm made points in my estimation.

L. L. Bean did the same thing one time when a pair of rubber-bottomed pacs I had ordered were cursed by improper stitching that blistered the feet. Although I had worn the shoes for a couple of weeks, prior to discovering the flaw, they were immediately exchanged at no cost. Old Leon Bean used to take great pride in his Maine hunting shoe, as his heirs still do, so there was no question.

Dozens of lesser firms—and some of the huge, sell-everything houses, such as Sears—offer a wide variety of practical tackle and ancillary equipment. The best of them, and I hold Sears a sterling example, are scrupulously honest in their dealings with customers. There is nothing very exotic about merchandise offered, but it is fairly priced and often well chosen by knowledgeable consultants.

An outlet to avoid is the one that plasters newspaper and cheap magazine pages with ads offering "complete fishing out-fits"—everything from rod, reel, and line down through an assortment of lures and a tackle box—for some ridiculously low figure. The merchandise is junk, a come on, and one of America's shames because such advertising too often preys on the ignorant and the disadvantaged.

Similarly, unless you're an incurable gambler, beware of direct mail "secret weapons" just invented and guaranteed to slaughter all game fishes. Curiously, it has been my observation that high-velocity advertising executives often prove patsies for this approach and are willing to spend healthy sums of money for a gimmick invented before they were born, and not too effective even then. Does it take a huckster to catch a huckster?

Secret weapons are pretty hard to come by. Trout, salmon, and other finny warriors are brought to account with time-tested tackle and skill in angling. The shortcuts usually turn out to be ancient lures or some rod–reel–line combination dreamed up by a nonfisherman with a fertile imagination, a slide rule, and an unsuspecting financial angel to pay the freight.

A friend of mine who can't be stupid, since he runs a multi-million dollar international business, admitted that he'd spent $25 for a "guaranteed lure." It sure was *that*, because it was a precise copy of an old spoon and feather contraption favored by southern black bass fishermen before Lucky Lindy ever thought of flying to Paris!

In its heyday the lure sold for less than a dollar. Yet, aside from "secret weapon" propaganda, the latter-day huckster couldn't be accused of warping facts. This artificial is truly guaranteed to catch fish. How many and how often is another matter. Nobody requires a consumer to purchase nonsense.

Wretched Mess News, a Rocky Mountain outdoor humor magazine, once publicized the worth of "genuine Madison

194

River throwing stones." It was a rib-tickling spoof, but a later promoter packaged "Pet Rocks" and sold a pile of them in flamboyant cardboard containers, for $4.95 apiece!

Almost every American city is graced by one or more cut-rate establishments, usually spacious hardware or department stores that feature sporting-goods counters. There are two basic types and, unfortunately, most of them are presided over by sharp young men or women who don't know the difference between a double-tapered fly line and a hank of sisal rope. Nor do they care, because the stuff has arrived in job lots and will be bargain priced. Generally, these firms offer no repair service and won't refund the price of an article found to be damaged, or won't replace said article.

This is changing. Competition for available trade steadily spawns cut-rate outlets manned by intelligent sales personnel who offer service and scorn the bamboozling of customers. The best never hesitate to replace a damaged item or refund money if the buyer is so inclined. Service in the way of repair leaves much to be desired, although some regularly arrange clinics where a factory representative presides for a day or so, rehabilitating his specific product for a modest fee or for nothing other than good public relations.

In any cut-rate shop an angler who knows precisely what he wants in the way of tackle or equipment may profit by browsing. There are definite bargains, for often an excellent item will be offered as a "leader," well below the usual suggested retail price. The sticker is a vast amount of inferior merchandise, obvious to an advanced angler but rarely spotted by an unschooled enthusiast. It is a disaster to go in cold and naive, yet shopping with the aid of a knowledgeable friend can turn up fine field grade—or even occasional classic articles —for less than the specialized sporting-goods shop can buy. Knowing manufacturer-jobber-dealer discounts, I have often found job-lot articles price tagged at pennies less than the middleman's cost.

Other articles, however, may be right up there with suggested retail price, and some higher. Cut rate doesn't always mean what it says.

As a rule of thumb, go to either the famous sporting-goods outfitters or to local specialists for the best in equipment. Trust the recognized mail-order houses for practical field-grade gear and fair prices. Shop cut-rate only if you are adequately informed and can recognize a bargain.

11

Trout on Ice

It would be misleading to say that I am an all-out advocate of ice fishing for trout, since I am not—and actually feel that these grand game fishes should be given a few months of peace in our frigid north country. However, tolerance is a virtue and anyone who rails against a sport that is both legal and soul-satisfying to others has troubles. I'll also have to admit that I've enjoyed occasional midwinter encounters and have never been known to scorn the silvery, hard-fleshed salmonids iced and later broiled over glowing coals.

For a number of years, back in the 50s and 60s, I lived in a house on the shore of a Massachusetts lake that was—and still is—liberally stocked with trout. Each long winter season it was possible for me to combine gainful labor and sport. I could assault a typewriter in warm comfort, yet keep a blood-shot eye focused on two or three little tie-ups (tilts) hooped like Arctic rat traps just outside a picture window. Our literature contains very little about ice fishing for salmonids, although a number of states permit the practice, hence I sought information as avidly as I did the odd rainbow or brown for breakfast.

My lake is situated in a near metropolitan suburb. In addition to the stocked trout, there are the usual schools of yellow perch, a few black bass and pickerel, plus bluegills, white perch, sunnies, crappies—and a healthy population of smelt. Off our digs we enjoyed rocky bottom, so browns and rainbows were there. Massachusetts allows only two per day during the cold-weather months, yet there was never any temptation to fracture the law since these fish didn't seem very hungry or active under an ice cover. I scratched for plunder and certain things became apparent.

Depth ranged to about 30 feet and each bait was positioned to probe a different level. Redfin shiners and angleworms were first offerings, although the latter never proved very effective and were finally phased out. Most surprising was the fact that a majority of trout preferred a relatively high-riding shiner to that worked right over bottom. Such a bait, wearily circling at 4 or 5 feet under the ice, usually invited attack. I never enjoyed fast action, maybe three or four flags during a long morning and afternoon.

All of the salmonids are cold-water fish, yet this must be qualified. Basic metabolism slows as temperatures plummet and many feed lethargically. None offer very stirring battle when hooked, since a handline is no-nonsense gear. Light and limber jigging sticks provide better sport, and there is a definite trend toward this tackle in many winter fishing areas. Some of the various species are far more accommodating than others.

On a scale progressing from hardest-to-please on up to most obliging, a frostbite angler finds rainbow and brown trout, in that order, elusive. Landlocked salmon, where the law allows, can be taken in fair numbers, and lake trout (togue) sustain a considerable winter fishery. Brook trout may be easiest of all to take through the ice or from an open stream. Once, before the law stepped in, lumberjacks were able to harvest a fearful toll in northern ponds during the winter months. You can collect squaretails regularly.

198

Where streams remain open, winter angling can be a rod and line adventure. It's a cold day, but here's a trophy fish on the Yellowstone River. (Photo by Erwin A. Bauer)

I recall, with a twinge of regret, a teen-age indiscretion. It wasn't spudding at all, but rather a December adventure. On the eve of a deer-hunting season I got all psyched up about the romance of "living off the land" and decided to poach some trout for a lunch in the woods.

It was very cold, with crusty snow and ponds frozen solid, but I always had some angleworms cached in a cellar holding box. Therefore, I repaired to a local stream and used a handline rather than a rod and reel. Nonchalantly attempting to look like a bird-watcher, I fed a worm-baited hook into the sucking current under an earthen dam.

A strike is indicated by the vertical flag. This is a modern underwater spool tilt or tip-up.

Immediately a little squaretail latched on and I hauled him out—still in fall spawning color and brilliantly tinted. Then another, and I had enough for a forbidden lunch on the following day. It would appall me to do such a thing now, but I guess I'm glad I did it then. Like all of the old outlaws, I was convinced that fish and game belonged to countrymen.

I didn't get my deer, and it served me right!

Ice-fishing gear and tactics have been vastly improved during the past couple of decades. There are two basic and practical ice-fishing methods in winter trout fishing, and both have evolved into fine arts. Equipment consists of tilts, plus jigging sticks. These are often used simultaneously, although one must consult local regulations governing the number of lines permitted per angler. Where state law allows five hooks in action, the sport who wants to copper his bets with a solo jigging rod must retire one of the positioned tilts.

A number of cleverly designed tip-ups are available on to-day's market, and the best are fitted with underwater reel spools to defeat a freeze-up. Above-water spools and the simple expedient of coiling running line on the ice get short shrift now, although such traps continue to see limited service. Briefly, each tilt is a device rigged with a spring-activated or counterweighted flag triggered by a strike. Each is set to present a bait at a predetermined depth, and the well-educated angler usually places spreads over ground known to harbor salmonids. Live baits are favored, although cut chunks often prove effective.

The first jigging sticks are said to have originated in Scandinavia and were rather crude by comparison with modern tackle. Traditional Swedish sticks, short lengths of carved wood, are still popular among rank-and-file anglers, but there is a current trend toward a far more sensitive and deadly instrument. This is usually a limber, abbreviated rod, often constructed from the tip section of a fly rod, fitted with a cork butt section and a reel seat. Instead of the twin prongs of the Scandinavian import, around which line is wound, a space-age tool will mount a free-spool reel filled with light monofilament line.

My own choice is the tip section of a fiberglass fly rod, about 3 feet long, and an Ambassadeur 5000 level-wind baitcasting reel filled with 4-pound-test mono. Free-spool permits swift presentation of a tiny lure, and a smooth star-drag—coupled to the short rod's resilience—guarantees a measure of sport in playing a determined fish. Various slip-cast reels and simple spools that can be controlled by the pressure of an index finger are commonly used.

My jigging rod is fitted with light but oversize ring guides and tiptop, the big rings chosen to defeat clogging by ice accumulation. Some fearfully efficient technicians insist upon a pierced rubber pencil eraser cemented or wound into the

You get there fast when a flag is sprung, hoping to hook a winter trout.

tiptop ring. Line is threaded through the tiny aperture and, of course, must be manually pulled off the reel's spool to allow presentation at proper depth. This is done to assure more delicate control in jigging, with no line bounce.

Nylon monofilament is the most practical line to use in jigging, and the lighter the strand the more efficient it will be. Color doesn't seem to matter as far as trout are concerned, although it can make a difference to the myopic angler.

An increasing number of tip-up jockeys also use mono, although most of the advanced practitioners still vote for Dacron or nylon braid, which offers a better hand-hold, remains limp in spite of subzero air temperatures, and works well with several feet of single-strand leader. Old-fashioned linen, or Cuttyhunk, is used, although its tendency to rot if not dried after use is a handicap.

First there must be ice, something often taken for granted after a quick freeze. The old and often tricky rule is that 1 inch of black ice will support a man, and 2 inches a horse. Don't count on it.

During the first period of hard freeze any small pond bereft of current or springholes will seal rapidly. Big lakes, swept by wind and current, resist winter's grip and should always be treated with respect. Even in midseason, with maybe 18 inches of solid covering, there can be pressure ridges that buckle upward and can trap a snowmobile or passenger car. It can be a mighty traumatic experience to scramble through the windows of a sedan as it crunches swiftly through a treacherous weak spot with 40 or 50 feet of black cold water below. This happens with nightmare frequency in the north country.

So-called "first ice" and "last ice" entrance winter anglers since salmonids often feed most avidly at either extreme. Therefore, the gamblers among us probe that first, thin black bonanza—and sortie again when the covering is dirty white and rubbery just prior to a spring breakup. These are times that may ensure limit catches, but they dictate cautious operation. Motor vehicles are best left ashore, the buddy system is wise, and each fisherman should tote a reasonable length of rope to use if a companion must be snaked out of trouble.

Proper clothing is essential to the sport, and nothing quite beats light woolens topped by goosedown parkas and pants, plus a shell windbreaker. By all means favor a hat that can be pulled down over the ears, or old-fashioned earmuffs. Gloves —although often discarded in the heat of action—are essential, and you'll want boots fitted with steel ice-creepers unless there's a snow cover.

Any winter day on a lake can be reasonably summerlike, but this is an exception. Usually the ice booms like distant artillery fire as it freezes, the wind is right out of the devil's ice box, and snow will be driving almost horizontally. It is well to remember that extra garments can be shed, but those left at home are of little use. Maybe you'll have a headquarters

Limber jigging sticks, often the tip section of a light fly rod, are increasingly favored by frostbite anglers.

campfire, and perhaps the exertion of spudding holes will raise a sweat. In youth, I always strapped on skates to provide warming exercise while tending a string of traps, and must admit standard frustration when the blades cut line coiled beside each of those old-fashioned tip-ups.

Trout on Ice

No great admirer of the snowmobile improperly used in wilderness country, that snarling little conveyance is a grand prime mover for a sled or toboggan stocked with tackle, lunches, and chisels or power augers. Light automobiles, where the covering is adequate, see much service, and a few million frostbite anglers still drag sleds or toboggans fitted with cargo boxes. On a small pond, or even on a big lake if you happen to be a hardy outdoorsman, a back pack or shoulder-slung duffel bag may be adequate.

Salmonids are not fond of noise. In shallow water, and particularly where there is a rocky bottom that acts as a sounding board, the thumping caused by spudding holes through the ice scatters the schools and may ensure lean fishing until some period of silence has been observed. In addition to laborless efficiency in boring through heavy covers, the power auger is reasonably quiet in operation. Chisels, still used by a majority of sportsmen and much in vogue while searching out concentrations of fish with a jigging stick, set up quite a subsurface racket, hence it is logical to retrace one's steps after spudding a line of holes to fish those that have been rested.

Profitable locations and depths are essential, the former a matter of prospecting and familiarity with bottom conformation. Ideal depth varies with the lake, the species, the season, and weather conditions. Any springhole loaded with smelt or other forage can be a prime choice, and such lodes are rarely advertised by regulars who have them pinpointed by triangulation. As well ask a woodcock or grouse hunter the coordinates of a hot corner!

Techniques vary with each species, but browns and rainbows are often found in upper levels over shoals. Lake trout can feed high or low and each lake's strike zone will depend on a depth level made most comfortable by temperature and oxygen content during a given season. This is also governed by forage available and the movement of resident bait. In any event, you'll want to determine depth as a first step. The old-fashioned and still practical sounding weight accomplishes the task well, and there are several portable electronic depth-finders that not only bounce sound waves off the bottom but can indicate schools of fish at any level.

Bob Boillard of Biddeford, Maine, and an advanced ice angler, stresses a prospecting technique used by many expert ice fishermen and sadly neglected by a host of beginners. "Having bored a hole through the ice, cover your head with a jacket or something else to shield out overhead light. If the water is clear you'll be able to check the type of bottom, rock, sand, or weed, and then see bait darting around. Believe me, bait will be attracted to the light streaming through that spud-hole, and you are likely to spot lake trout and salmon drawn to the schooling bait."

Brown, rainbow, and squaretail trout are often found near the shore, especially close to a shoal drop-off, and a springhole loaded with smelt is equally attractive. If there is a question of depth, and for some unknown reason often there is, initiate a campaign by fishing a different level with each tip-up line, from perhaps 5 feet under the ice down to rock bottom. Once the payoff range is discovered, all lines can be positioned in a strike zone.

Boillard's terminal tackle is light, and this is par for the course among all advanced winter trout hunters. A light leader is employed, secured to the running line via a tiny snap swivel. A single BB shot is attached at the 3-foot mark, followed by two or three small red, white, or yellow beads serving as stops. There is another miniature snap swivel, 18 inches of monofilament, and a short-shanked claw hook in size 6 to 8. Running line on the tilt's underwater spool is 15- to 20-pound-test braid, and Bob likes Cortland Micron. Any of the better braids in similar tests work well. The package lacks overpowering strength, yet it produces far better than brute clout. Small hooks allow nearly unfettered bait movement and the careful playing of fish ensures success. Some specialists forego colored beads as terminal tackle stops and use a couple of pearl-plastic shirt buttons instead.

Bait is normally a small shiner, a smelt where the law permits, or perhaps a tomcod. These can be hooked through the skin of the back just ahead of the dorsal fin or—Boillard's preference—through the edges of the lips, from the top down through. The presentation is delicate, to allow the bait as much freedom as possible and to keep it lively over a considerable period of time. Tilt triggering devices must be sensitive, yet not so hair trigger that they wind-flag.

Where lake trout are the quarry, depth varies from shoal to very deep. Togue are prone to forage in shallows, over rocky shoals, and also in black depths. They are active throughout the year and have hearty appetites. Strike zones vary in different waters and seasons, sometimes just under the ice if smelt are swarming there, and again down to 50 or 100 feet. Prime time usually occurs just prior to the arrival of a warming weather front, especially when this ends a deep-freeze period.

Boillard's carefully maintained logs indicate that fastest action is likely from about one-half hour after sunrise to, say, 10 A.M., with another peak period building from 3 P.M. to sunset. "However," he admits ruefully, "this schedule can be shot full of holes. If it happens to be warm, overcast, with rain or fog in a thaw, they may feed all day."

High-level togue fishing has one unfortunate aspect, particularly where landlocked salmon are present and protected by law. The salmon will forage right under an ice cover and, although carefully released, may be injured by occasional deep hooking. No problem where a state's fisheries regulations permit a small limit of handsome landlocks.

Live baits proved to be most successful on lake trout include shiners, smelt, tomcod, and chubs. Many consider small suckers exceptionally good. Chumming is often practiced— openly where the law allows and surreptitiously otherwise. This, however, is usually done when a jigging stick is employed. Then, while the jig is sweetened with a tail section of smelt, shiner, or whatever, the forward portion is cut into bits and allowed to filter into the depths as a come-on.

An ice fisherman, like every other angler on earth, must be something of an opportunist. Sometimes, when lake trout are slow to take live baits on tilt-lines, they fall all over themselves to grab a jigged lure. These can be almost any of a variety that flash when raised or lowered, and prime examples include the Swedish Pimple, Hopkins, and Kastmaster types. A lot of specialists make their own and swear by a variety of finishes such as chrome, gold, copper, or combinations of metallic and color.

Togue, like other salmonids, will take jigs that are unsweetened, yet often prefer a bit of shiner or smelt—say 1 to 2 inches of the tail section. There may well be a scent-taste factor at work here but, regardless, one never argues with success. Naturally, the jigging stick is most efficiently used in relatively shoal water, since it seems a turtle's age while a tiny jig flutters down to deep bottom.

Where conditions permit with any of the trout clan, it can be highly rewarding to spud a jig hole close to a tip-up location, perhaps 4 to 8 feet away. Both rigs seem to get more attention, perhaps because the flash of the lure draws cruising gamesters into the payoff area.

Browns, rainbows, and squaretails are partial to many small tidbits attached to a tiny hook on a jigging spoon. These include the time-honored perch eye, an inch of angleworm, various grubs, and pickled salmon eggs—as well as smidgeons of cut smelt and shiner. They will take the artificial sans bait, but rarely so often.

Each spudding enthusiast has his own jigging technique, yet there is a rough pattern. A lure is allowed to plummet all the way to bottom, then raised a foot or so and manipulated by a raising and lowering of the rod's tip. Often it is deemed wise to follow this with slow jigging at various depths all the way to the surface, but lure action remains important.

That action is the point where great minds differ slightly: some prefer a cadenced, almost metronomelike action, a sort of one-two-three second count in jigging, followed by a pause of five to fifteen seconds. Some are aggressive, continually moving the lure. Many regularly raise it 4 to 5 feet off bottom and then let it drop back. I have watched a few highly successful lads who interspersed the up and down motion with no more than a trembling of the tip. The technique that works on one day may not be so effective on another, so experimentation is worthwhile.

Things hard to explain are rather commonplace. For example, a spoon that is fluttering free while dropping into the depths may be savagely attacked. There is no strike felt, but the clever jig-man knows what has happened because there is an instant pause in the descent of his line, so he switches the tip and a trout is on. Sometimes it also pays to let a jig lie still on the bottom for several seconds; then, as it is slowly brought in an inch or so toward the light, a fish will attack. He's obviously seen it descend, watches the thing curiously, and wallops it when it moves.

Artificial lures have yet to progress beyond a few favored types. Ice flies, usually soft-hackled with built-in weight, can be useful, but the most productive remain small, streamlined metal flashers. Ken Gebhardt of Peekskill, New York, used a miniature Swedish Pimple with a small piece of minnow tail for bait to ice a 11 pound, 1 ounce brown trout at the West Branch Reservoir in Durham County, New York, on February 15, 1975. The fish was a handsome, full-bodied specimen, 30 inches long.

Gebhardt's tactics are very similar to those employed by Bob Boillard and other aces on ice. He uses a "cut-down one-quarter-ounce-rated bait-casting rod with a Luxor open-face spinning reel, 6-pound-test Bonnyl line, a small Sampo snap, and a Swedish Pimple lure sweetened with shiner tail.

"The jig is let all the way down to the bottom, then cranked up about 2 feet and jigged, with the tip moving about 6 inches every few seconds. This is usually the hot spot. We will work our way up to the top in about 5-foot intervals, then do it all over again. We usually drill ten or so holes apiece until we get some action. If possible," again a warning sounded by all serious winter trout hunters, "drill with an ice auger, as a spud pounding its way through the ice seems to alarm trout. Oddly enough, our jigging seems to be best during the bright portions of the day when the tip-ups are dead."

So far as I know, Boillard and Gebhardt have never met or corresponded, yet their approach is almost identical. Ken uses the same terminal tackle in tip-up fishing, right down to the split shot 18 inches above a size 6 or 8 hook—the same bait, the same general tactics.

"In fishing for trout," Ken declares, "we have found them to be either just off the bottom or just under the ice, rarely in between. Why this disparity in depth I don't know. More often they are deep and then we rig two or three tip-ups so that the minnow is about 3 feet above bottom. The other one or two (we are allowed five tip-ups in New York) are fished with only the leader and perhaps a couple of feet of line out, no split shot.

"With tip-ups 90 percent of the action on trout is at dawn and for about an hour after, plus a smaller 'bite' at dusk. It helps, of course, if you know the lake, the ledges, rockpiles, and other structure. Best, and these spots are guarded like gold mines, are springholes. These always harbor quantities of trout and are usually productive all day long.

"There is a way of finding these holes with reasonable accuracy, even on a strange lake if you can be there when it is beginning to freeze over and there is perhaps an inch of ice formed. Look for small open patches of water, open for a reason other than a current—unlikely in a small lake—but due to a gaggle of Canada geese easy to spot, or the warmer water of a spring.

"This technique is only useful in the very beginning, as the lake soon freezes solid. After you locate such a hole and make a note of its location by using at least three ranges, write the information down in a notebook. The old way of seeing who

Ice fishermen working small lakes and ponds often tote equipment in boxes attached to sleds. Snowmobiles are favored for the long haul.

is catching fish, and where, is just as valid on the ice as in the salt chuck."

Arguments have raged, and will continue to splutter, about the ethics involved in ice fishing for trout. Many summer snipers feel that the game should be outlawed on the basis that salmonids are too precious to be winched out of a deep-freeze. I must admit to sympathy with the boys of summer, yet it's probably academic since modern fisheries management strives to prohibit any rape of a renewable resource. Sportfishing is as much people management as fish management: if X number of recreation hours can be provided at minimal cost, without harming the trout population, then we must smother our latent patrician emotion and accept majority rule.

Besides, the game is a lot of fun. I like a cold sting of winter air and the suspense involved. I dote on a headquarters campfire ashore and the aroma of hamburgers sizzling on a grill while all of the troops keep a collective eye on tilts carefully positioned. No strike on a jigged lure is quite so thrilling as a trout's rise to a fly, but it sure stimulates a flow of adrenaline.

I guess I like it—and I certainly like the fringe benefits, such as a hearty meal after action, a glass of something tinkly, and applewood blazing in a fireplace. You can get pretty sleepy that way, and it's healthy.

12

The Killers

Imagine this North American continent before white men arrived: It was a place of unbelievable abundance, of lakes and rivers alive with fish, a virgin wilderness peopled by tribes of aborigines who warred among themselves, but respected earth's largesse. The land, the water, the game, and the fishes belonged to all, not to a chosen few, and there were no rapacious industries to destroy natural resources.

Deterioration of a delicate ecosystem began when it was rudely disrupted by a new culture and philosophy. This almost total war on the environment escalated through the nineteenth century, reaching its horrendous peak in the years just prior to and following World War II. Then, in the late 50s, Rachel Carson came along to sound a warning with her emotional and well-researched *Silent Spring*. Citizens began to man the barricades and insist upon prudence. For the first time in the history of America, we collectively rebelled against the senseless destruction of natural resources. Was it too late?

Not necessarily. The Bonny Brook I mentioned earlier is gone, swallowed up and defiled by industry. All of us recall our own bonny brooks, and know that we can't resurrect

Competition is the word where fishing pressure builds to hectic proportions. This is dawn of opening day on a well-stocked central Massachusetts lake.

them. We *can* war against future desecration, if the enemy is singled out, remorselessly attacked and defeated. Times haven't changed so much. Greed is still there, and if we allow the exploiters free rein, then the killers are you and me!

Our pioneers had no inkling of the forces they set in motion. Or, perhaps, they would have shrugged off eventual chaos since there was money to be made. If that is so, the trend of thought survives—evident in the planning of amoral engineers who would sacrifice entire blocks of the ecosystem for the sake of energy generated by a power plant that will utterly destroy a once productive estuary or river, and in the designs of developers and industrialists who see the immediate dollar sign, but not the death that follows a flagrant disregard for life-giving nature. Nobody rails against healthy progress, yet there must be a valid compromise.

Trout are important to those of us who enjoy angling, but trout are unimportant if this Andromeda Strain of destruction without replacement—which began more than 200 years ago and burgeoned in the twentieth century—continues. It is a gamble with all life, including that of the human being. Trout may be likened to the canaries once used (and maybe still used) in coal mines: when they succumb, men are in peril.

Sport fishermen, together with hunters, have been made whipping boys in the steady decline of our natural resources, yet it has always been the ruthless desecrations of industry and the lava flow of cement, steel, and pollutants that hasten a silent spring. No native digger, no hunter of past or present has ever massacred his environment. This despicable act has always been the work of a new and conquering power intent on ignoring every rule of nature to exploit a weaker people, a land mass, a very environment for the sake of plunder and profit.

In many states it is illegal to pick certain endangered wild-flowers, and this may be prudent legislation. However, it is *not* illegal to bulldoze off an entire hillside, riotous with endangered flowers, for a parking lot or supermarket; nothing will ever grow there again.

If there is a wetland, it is considered a waste unless filled; if a trout stream, it is fed into plastic pipes, channelized or diverted. City Hall decides, and City Hall, whether town, state, or federal, is pretty hard to beat. More than one-fifth of all Americans are government workers, and the word goes around. No threats, simply a reminder that the job is good—and we'd like your vote on this issue. They get the vote.

A rape of natural resources continues, now hopefully slowed by citizen outrage and accumulated knowledge about what must happen in a foreseeable future if pillage remains unchecked. Yet, so long as cautious state and federal agencies levy fines that can be written off in a rush of profit, some industries will ignore vague, hardly enforceable laws. Politicians too often break trail for the spoilers, and there are many American sportsmen who lose by default, not by intent. These are the well-meaning folk who attend local club meetings, have a few drinks, make a great noise at monthly meetings, and then subside into silence. They do not contact state and federal lawmakers when destructive bills are introduced, and then they wonder why legislators do not vote in their favor.

Sure, lots of chiefs break their lances leading crusades, and then all of the sycophants applaud while screaming: "Give 'em hell, boy, we're right behind you!"

But they're not; they are figuratively 3,000 miles back where there is no shellfire and no iron rations. A few even sell their fellows short by pandering to state officials who promise a truckload of hatchery trout for a local pond.

Our media, by and large, treat hunting and fishing as poor relatives and wax eloquent about spectator sport. A few of the big metropolitan newspapers award scant space to highly qualified outdoor writers, and then run front-page stories applauding antigun, antiangling minority groups. Many of the nation's smaller newspapers print weekly or sometimes daily columns written by local aficionados. Some of these are surprisingly good, and some are beyond redemption. Payment, usually, is far less than a living wage, so the rod and gun writer's strip amounts to a part-time hobby. Newsprint still reaches a majority of Americans and can sway public opinion. Therefore, if sportsmen want a fair shake with accurate reporting, then they must demand it.

Canadians have an intense desire to protect their Atlantic salmon rivers. Boston angler Dr. Charles Storey plays a grilse on Quebec's Grand River.

To date, network TV has exhibited an astonishing disregard for fact. There, chairborne city types look for something spectacular and are willing to warp the truth in a so-called documentary. "Guns of Autumn," in the fall of 1975, was a typical example: it covered the minority excesses of hunters, but pictured little of majority sportsmanship and concern. As a fictitious tearjerker, the telecast succeeded, yet truth was not in it.

Trout addicts should not assume that they are safe and beyond the spiteful attack of antihunting zealots. Cleveland Amory has publicly stated that his group wants to end all gunning in America, and then terminate the "cruelty of sportfishing." At this writing the Humane Society of the United States is distributing a pamphlet aimed at children, urging the kids to call for an end to fishing. "When they've begun to THINK," the publication declares, "many grown-ups who used to fish have given it up, and now instead of killing, they find fun in studying fish just as Chuang Tse did."

Why mention such curious trends of thought in a book about trout hunting? For the simple reason that sportsmen and serious environmentalists are locked in a deadly battle with groups of well-funded zealots who employ emotion, warped reasoning, and blatant propaganda (including this attempt to brainwash children) in their attempt to attain utopia. An angler may shrug it off as insane raving, yet it remains his duty to rebut.

Incredibly, there are state divisions of fisheries and game that knuckle under to do-gooders by forgetting their mandate. The very terms "fish and game" or "hunting and fishing" are being phased out of the language by frightened public servants. Now it is "fisheries and wildlife" or "department of ecology." By some semantic little twist of the language, we are urged to believe that no rod or gun is involved. Ludicrous? Maybe, but consider developments.

Almost always the license dollars of anglers and gunners fund such agencies. Sportsmen pay for the management of fish and game, yet they often get a plethora of make-work research in other fields. Outdoorsmen generally adore flowers and songbirds, they entertain no aversion to bats, salamanders, spiders, and venomous snakes that exist in a wild environment —but they *pay* for professional management of fish and game.

Adoption of an all-inclusive program places too great a work load on dedicated fisheries and wildlife biologists, and funding becomes nearly impossible unless the general public agrees to share a burden, which it usually will not. Even if a state's general funds are allocated to a fish and game division, there is peril. Politics enter the lists and bona-fide technicians can't make their own decisions. Use of general funds can be considered a narcotic solution, an addiction impossible to kick. If the politicians provide funds, they rule. Then it becomes a scatter-shot approach replete with patronage, which places incompetents above qualified personnel simply because said incompetents are willing to prostitute themselves. Where this occurs, well-trained biologists either resign or accept the status quo because there is no way out.

There are still many good and true administrators, but the present trend may make them members of an endangered species. Check your own state agency and see whether it orders technicians to "prove" things long known to be unprovable, whether it funds projects that have little to do with angling or gunning, whether it regularly applauds those who would unjustly curtail the sport you pay for.

It is not too late for a return to common sense, nor has the time passed to build a viable society without destroying an environment. England, old as its mossy shrine at Stonehenge and a kingdom where the industrial revolution prospered, still protects clean, cold streams. I have seen trout finning placidly in German rivers coursing through the centers of towns where smokestacks belched. If they can do it, we can.

Horizons recede because we are a permissive people. There is good trout fishing throughout America, but not the cornucopia of fond memory. Near-metropolitan waters are pounded, as they must be, and native fish are both small and wary. The literature extols places now as ravaged as ancient Troy, and we attempt to breathe life into wonderlands long degenerated into Disneylands.

My own New England is a pretty good example. This was, for a lengthy span of years, "the northwoods." You came up here prepared to battle grand fishes, and usually found them. Now condolences are in order and public-relations laborers struggle to preserve an image. Our vacation states levy back-breaking nonresident license fees, and it's really nonsense because they have little to offer. The wave of tourism passes northward; today a visiting angler can find better sport in the Canadian bush, and pay less.

So there is a branching out, a constant search for new lodes. In our northeast the adventurer heads for Canada's still largely virgin bush. In the United States trout fishing moves westward, and that was entirely predictable in view of eastern deterioration. Jackson Hole, Wyoming, and Livingston, Montana, are now jumping-off spots. Facetiously, but with more truth than humor, I have suggested that the address of any well-known trout fisherman in midsummer would have to be: Wallfish #H23-J, c/o Dan Bailey's Fly Shop, Livingston, Montana.

Count it view-with-alarm if you choose, but the western angler had best arm himself against the self-destructing sophistry of the East. The grandest of rivers can be transformed into running sewers by too much humanity, and a lush jungle of outdoor literature triggers the assault.

Now we enjoy an affluent society, many of whose members are wealthy enough to board the big jets and travel. Scandinavia, New Zealand, the Argentine, and Chile all lie within scant hours of New York and Los Angeles. Alaska and northern Canada are opening up, thanks to rapid air transportation and the foreloopers who serve as outfitters and guides—first the native pathfinder, and then the promoter; first wall tents, then a plush lodge followed by a string of camps ridgepole to ridgepole.

Finally the roads go in, and that is the end, because it is no longer back-of-beyond. A man no longer has to sweat for his goodies: he'll have his gin mills and pizza palaces, bowling alleys and gourmet restaurants. There'll be rigidly controlled campgrounds where advance reservations are required. There won't be many trophy fish.

Today's ultimate solution is to board a bush plane and fly over the far mountain into a paradise that is still distant from

Erwin A. Bauer, one of America's foremost outdoor writers and an expert angler, nets a Madison River brown trout. (Photo by Erwin A. Bauer)

civilization. There will be no comfortable lodges or tap water, just the lovely, brooding land and brawling streams, plus a couple of taciturn guides who won't even bother to swat no-see-ums or mosquitoes. The fishing will be superlative and, if you're a candidate for a rubber-lined room—like so many of us who are outdoor writers—then you may even write an epic story about it.

Once, long ago, I helped to kill a trout pond. It wasn't intentional murder because I didn't even know that the act had been committed until a year had passed and reports of homicide trickled back through a sorrowful grapevine. The place was Snake Pond, up and beyond Grand Lake Mattagamon in Maine, and it was remote at the time, reached only by a wilderness canoe trip or airplane. We flew, of course.

I don't know how long three of us camped, maybe four or five days, but we were all alone mimicking the screams of the loons, examining bear tracks in the mud, catching legions of big trout and releasing all but a few of the smaller ones reserved for meals. That was the greatest squaretail trout fishing I ever saw in the continental United States, with trophies up to just about 6 pounds. We came out of there insect bitten and ecstatic, and then I made one of the great errors of a misspent lifetime—I wrote about it.

Not just locally, but an article for *Outdoors Magazine*, now defunct, then well read. I blueprinted the entire expedition and submitted a batch of photos. I think they paid me $100 to be a Judas.

A year later I received a mournful card from Maine guide Chubb Foster. He said: "Snake Pond now looks like headquarters for Richthofen's Flying Circus and it is being fished out." Everybody wanted in, and everybody got in via the little float planes.

I felt like a traitor and my conscience was only partially healed a couple of seasons later when a lumber company pushed a road through. After that, of course, the end was inevitable—there is no great fishing on the track of internal combustion.

This is par for the course. I have been guilty, and so have a majority of outdoor writers who must tell the truth and level with their readers, yet in doing so they kill the thing they love. We destroy wilderness and solitude and innocence. Then the path is worn smooth, the litter accumulates, and the fish are pounded. A partial solution is to publicize vast bodies of water while remaining vague about smaller, more fragile streams and ponds.

Publicity can be deadly, quite as lethal in a small, heavily populated suburban township as it is in a wilderness. If, for example, a where-they're-hitting report notes that "Pine Tree Creek was stocked on Monday and has been producing limit catches for those in the know," then Pine Tree Creek will be a battleground the day after this information is printed.

Small streams and glistening little ponds can be trampled to death—and are. Big rivers and major lakes are harder to destroy, yet if the roads go in they will get a bad case of speedboat treatment. A lot of outdoor reporters know just how deadly the pinpoint can be, so they discuss general area, perhaps adding that "Trout fishing is excellent in Washington County now and Quill Gordon has been the best dry fly. Trollers like the Black Ghost, and spincasters are catching them on Mepp's Spinners." It's all accurate, and that is the story—sans precise directions for the multitudes. Therefore, no murderous concentration on a single stream or pond.

The reader who devours tidbits of information about hot spots unaccountably hates an outdoor writer's guts for blowing the whistle on one of his own favorites. Pipelines dry up as local experts keep their own counsel and smile benignly while refusing to divulge anything of interest. A qualified writer, whether assigned to the police beat or outdoor sport, must protect his sources while publishing all that is fit to print. It is a tight-rope operation, an accurate assessment of that which happens, coupled with some reluctance to provide blueprints for crowds.

Entire areas can be hurt by excessive publicity. My lifelong business has been marine angling and many peg me as a surfcaster whose major stamping ground is Cape Cod in Massachusetts. I have fished on many seas and have paid my dues in sweet water. The Cape was indeed dear to me, not only its rumbling surf, but a great many clean, cold little trout ponds, and I shamelessly promoted them.

Now I am almost loath to visit the narrow land, because traffic is vicious and waters are crowded. Night and day the boats whiz back and forth like a Gold Cup preliminary and there is no peace. Where twenty years ago I was a welcome promoter, now I am just another bit of human flotsam, prodded and regulated by the rangers of National Seashore and the janissaries of local townships who desire to make a buck on the bay.

National wilderness parks would seem to be one answer to the need for preservation, yet too often the concept is aborted. If a grand acreage of forest and stream could be acquired and left alone, that would be constructive. Often it doesn't work because each park becomes a federal make-work project. Immediately, upon acquisition, administration buildings, museums, bicycle trails, nature walks, and observation towers are constructed. Paved parking lots and reserved-site campgrounds are added.

Quickly, a great company of administrators and rangers descend on this "gem that is to be preserved in its wilderness state," and public-relations personnel grind out reams of copy dedicated to decoying the multitudes. Coney Island development may be held at bay, but government quite as thoroughly makes this land and water a business enterprise.

The "wilderness preserved" can become a federal Disneyland, still beautiful in a way, but peopled by throngs of enforcement folk, summer workmen planting shrubbery, repairing facilities, harvesting litter, and trying to maintain the estate. Politically oriented administrators are always afraid of the scornful few who arrive to strew garbage, destroy vegetation, intimidate decent citizens, or even burn the shingles torn off administration buildings. An honest angler may be penalized for his unintentional violations, but this shambling sea of lemmings is appeased by social scientists backed by gutless state and federal government.

Blame is not easily placed. Part of it is local greed for the tourist dollar, and part is government's insatiable desire to build patronage empires. Administrators come and go, shifted from one location to another, often bound by directives out of Washington written in gobbledygook by appointees who never saw the living color on a fish.

Although hard-fished by residents and tourists, Maine and New Hampshire yield trout and landlocked salmon. Dick Woolner's the angler here.

During the past few decades it has become evident that even the storehouses of the sea can be depleted, so it would seem obvious that inland trout—far less in numbers and more accessible—cannot long endure exploitation. Certainly it is a public right to enjoy angling, yet the public remains a collective killer through demanding excessive bag limits in many states. The salmonids are too precious for that.

In America, we simply cannot afford heavy kills of trout. While a minority of reverent, skilled anglers release far more than they keep, vociferous crowds shout for long seasons and bulging creels. This leads to a quantity rather than quality approach, making the attrition far too taxing.

All salmonids, in varying degrees, are excellent table fishes. Grumble about regarding a handsome trout as a food item if you choose, but remember that the local supermarket now charges about $2.00 for a chunk of commercial haddock just big enough to feed a child with no appetite. If the big catch is legal, and often it is, those who take limit catches day after day are entirely within their rights.

Little can be said for the greed that counts victory in successive hauls of fish as a sort of status symbol, often aggravated by the fact that these trout are not even brought to a fisherman's table, but are given away to admiring friends or even allowed to wind up in a garbage can because the "expert" rodsman is too lazy to dress them out and ensure utilization. There are, sorrowfully, a few who boast about tremendous kills. America cannot stand this much longer.

By participating in the exploitation of a very limited natural resource, or even by sanctioning with silence such depredation, we share a measure of blame. We have made our mistakes; we must admit our errors and correct them.

I won't beg off because I am an outdoor writer. As a group, we have a bad track record; we have disclosed secrets and secret places that should have remained inviolate. In too many cases we have promoted for the amoral tourist agencies and so-called area development. Some of us have even sold our questionable talent to cynical industry. Who ever said that journalists are members of the second-oldest trade on earth?

That's nonsense. We came first . . .

13

Tomorrow, and Tomorrow

As the fictional airpline pilot said to his passengers: "First the bad news, and then the good. We're lost, but we're making fine time!"

American trout fishermen aren't lost: they're just in the position of Dan'l Boone who admitted to being "bewildered on occasion." There is a new and viable spirit in resource management, much of it due to national concern about a swiftly deteriorating environment, much due to a banding together of sportsmen who have finally recognized a need for concerted action. It is necessary to reassess the facts, to resist old-crock belief, and to go forward.

Trout are precious and they require clean water. This may sound like a declaration that sunshine sustains life, yet many of us continue to take game fish for granted and assume that there will always be another stream unpolluted. Sorrowfully, there are just so many streams and so many trout. Industry unchecked soon fouls bright water. Humanity is a pollutant unless rigidly controlled.

It is necessary to organize, not solely on the provincial local level, but nationally. This is being done by such dedicated associations as the Isaak Walton League and Trout Unlimited. There are other groups quite as high-minded and they are aided by a few specialized magazines. If the effort has been less than successful in past years, there must be a reason. I suggest it has been an ancient ill—a division of forces.

Distasteful as it may be to purists, they are members of a minority. Ninety percent of American trout fishermen, at a guess, eschew fly casting and are hurt by a rather constant put down. Our literature generally regards bait and hardware anglers as second-class citizens, yet they comprise the big battalions that must be mobilized. We are not dealing with the supposed niceties of angling: we are talking about the very survival of trout!

Therefore, if fishermen are eager to save their sport, the first step is a reversal of current sophistry. We can no longer afford the polarization that results from any holier-than-thou dedication to fly casting. To win we need mass, not driblets.

It isn't enough to prate sportsmanship and release, since a mass of citizens can rightly argue that killing is ethical if the law says it is. The great goal will be achieved when all of us, fish-for-fun or fish-for-limits, engage in a common cause to ensure a heritage.

I don't think that fly-fishing-only or strict fish-for-fun will ever work. To arbitrarily take a stream or pond, or any part of either, and declare that it is off-limits to all but purists is class legislation. Baitmen and hardware merchants can cite logic in holding this unfair, since they buy a majority of licenses to support management of the fishery. It might be asked whether, if such legislation were adopted, flycasters should not be barred from waters open to the average sportsman who legally employs everything in his considerable arsenal?

Fish-for-fun seems utopian, since it entails releasing each and every trout brought to net or, in some cases, might allow the creeling of one or two. In addition to the aforementioned conflict between everyday anglers and purists, there are problems. Aquatic biologists remain divided over the plan for the simple reason that a healthy renewable resource is often dependent on a planned harvest. There can be wastage if overpopulation leads to stunting or disease. There is no such thing as a stockpiling of fish or game.

High-minded but questionably practical plans such as these do not strike to the heart of the matter—which is good management of a natural resource through clean water and either the natural propagation of native trout or the introduction of hatchery strains bred to survive in a natural environment. Fishing method, under law, is difficult to legislate unless every citizen is treated equally. It is no good to say "this river is for purists, and you hunkies can go elsewhere," for that is a form of feudalism.

Nonetheless, all arguments are nullified if we do not admit that there are not enough trout to permit wholesale harvesting. It doesn't matter whether these treasures are reduced to possession via a fly or a gob of angleworms—once killed and bedded in fern, they are gone. Academic anglers can wrangle endlessly over methods, while ignoring the law of supply and demand, but the problem won't be solved until certain actions are taken.

Perhaps the way to ensure equality and preserve a heritage is to limit, and limit drastically, the number of salmonids that can be killed on a given day. Granting this a first step, far less important than the ultimate preservation of bright waters and the cleansing of those now fouled, it is a thing that can be done without any expenditure of license dollars. Limiting the catch not only helps to maintain a trout population, it emphasizes the value of these regal fishes and constitutes basic wildlife management.

For various reasons, some of them logical, there is now a trend to allow trout fishing the year around. It has worked in some southern states and in a few northern areas as well, yet there are valid arguments against the practice. Surely year-round angling, intelligently controlled, should have little ad-

Western Maryland's Youghiogheny River, much of its length public property, is one of the finest trout streams in the state. (Photo by Lefty Kreh)

verse effect on the fishery; on the contrary, it might be a conservation measure because it would cancel out the fevered anticipation of an opening day.

Anglers are dreamers and part of the magic is anticipation. Any grand opening, regardless of attending crowds, is a zero hour to be treasured by those who find sleep difficult on the night prior to assault. Sure, ice may form in the rod guides and perhaps trout will not oblige, yet it is a beginning, a moment to adore even though ponds and streams are lined with enthusiasts, each mesmerized by a promise. Usually, some logy, emaciated beauties are winched to shore or boat. Everyone enjoys the outing, and that's the way it should be. It is Opening Day—and nothing like this will ever happen again.

So it follows that an administrator of sport fisheries must be cold and calculating. A short closed season builds anticipation. People who may never become ardent anglers get all psyched up, and they buy licenses. The money pays for research, management, and stocking. We may be idealists, but trout are expensive and it is still necessary to get the buck up.

There are possible handicaps. If you have a politically oriented division of fisheries and game—and very often this is the case in the heavily populated states—then the all-year season is made to order for tricksters in command. They may report regular, systematic stocking, but there are no checks and balances. Figures mean nothing, since a million fingerlings touted as "catchables" can be cited in press releases. Where there is fairly massive stocking prior to an opening day, citizens monitor the operation and observe the size and quality of fish going in. It isn't perfect, but it keeps people reasonably honest.

It is conceivable that ice fishing for trout must be eliminated or more rigidly controlled. Today's frostbite gladiator is often allowed to set five tip-ups. He is, if we go to definitions, a trapper and not an angler. Safety-wise, late winter ice regularly drowns enthusiastic gamblers who keep spudding until the cover is rubbery and dangerous. Such casualties provide ammunition for those who would eliminate all angling.

There are no universal blueprints and there are concepts proved false, but espoused by pressure groups. There is the folly of stockpiling. Trout, like men, live and die at appointed times and a given body of water can support a calculated poundage of fish flesh, no more. We seek, hopefully, a safe, renewable harvest. Therefore it is necessary to limit our assault well below a point of deadly attrition, and then seek a perpetuation of remaining suitable water, plus a clean-up of now defiled streams.

231

Aside from limiting the number of hooks in use at one time, or banning the poacher's spear or net, there is almost no way to regulate sporting tackle, nor is there present need. Techniques can be questionable, good for cracker-barrel argument, and frequently some maverick makes himself unpopular by citing evidence of a purist's unwitting drive to kill with kindness.

Examine, for openers, ultralight gear. At times you will fish ·fine leaders and spiderweb lines or you will not succeed—but the fish may suffer. A trout or salmon wrestled ashore in a hurry is still vibrantly alive and may well survive that traumatic experience after release. One literally bored to death by a long struggle against light pressure is pretty sure to be broken in body and spirit. Very light tackle, in the hands of an expert, is deadly. We have all sorts of learned treatises on casualties, but it's all guesswork. There are no hard statistics on the survival of trout that have been beaten to exhaustion and then turned loose.

It will be stated, with conviction and a healthy measure of fact, that the fine tippet required to present a tiny fly on a clear stream during the low water months offers a supreme challenge and that many of the sizable trout raised and hooked on such gossamer strands lose no time in breaking off. The hook, usually lightly imbedded, is soon keyholed out. In any event nobody, or at least very few of us, needs to catch trout for food. We had better be kind to them, else our children may never enjoy one of mankind's finest sports.

Sportsmanship, itself, is variously defined. I have personally released Atlantic salmon that should have been kept for the camp larder or for my table because they were bleeding and doomed. I did not release them of my own accord, but because I was a guest on a classic beat and had been firmly, if graciously, advised to turn them loose. I did, even though the local guide rolled his eyes and muttered obscenities about waste.

There is the opposite approach, a shameless desire to kill, most evident in the beginner who yearns for trophies to dis-

Trout stocking in the populous East is an event before the spring fishing season begins. Anglers gather to see trout released by state hatchery personnel.

play in an evening happy hour. Worse, many a guide or lodge owner wants heavyweights to display and photograph on a rack. Outdoor magazines now deemphasize the big string, yet some tackle manufacturers still debase the game with ads featuring dead meat.

Marine angling, during the past three decades, has led all of the greedy legions in such promotion. Ernie Lyons of Stuart, Florida, a grand conservationist and a sensitive writer, tells how early charter skippers outmaneuvered first efforts to tag and release sailfish. They'd professionally bill the handsome creature and, with a swift movement of muscular arms, break its back over the gunwale. Then, turning to the nonplussed angler, they'd exclaim: "Too bad! The fish died just as I lifted it out of the water."

A lot of salmonids die just that way, and it doesn't matter how they are caught. Those of us who prefer the fly are not angels—we have been known to stumble, too. But public opinion is swiftly turning against wastage. Even on salt water, charter skippers who insist on racking numbers of fish for promotional purposes draw an increasing measure of scorn. Release, marine or inland—after the swift snapping of a photo or two on the scene of action—has become the mark of a sportsman. There remains a need for education.

Americans are of all ethnic origins and our tastes vary, yet there is one thing that we all agree upon, and that is equality under the law. It doesn't always work and there are ample evidences of backsliding. However, special privilege is abhorrent and we are not going to recognize any knightly order over lesser breeds.

Anglers are increasingly well informed about fisheries dynamics, so the amoral politician abusing an administration of fisheries and game finds it more difficult to hoodwink license-holders. Where inept management and make-work research proliferate, the citizens know and coolly dissent. They work at grass-roots level, borers in the wood, rusting the crown and sword of self-appointed czars. Gradually, and on a national level, sportsmen are organizing.

We still see sociological stocking, but it is tremendously expensive and it is wrong, politically contrived to satisfy the wishes of voters in heavily populated areas. The obscenity caters to a tourist industry, too, where it is deemed necessary to pump hatchery trout or exotics into a given water.

Certainly put-and-take stocking will continue so long as there is demand and costs do not soar right out of orbit. If sportsmen in metropolitan areas and heavily populated states vote to foot the bill, that is fair enough—although it is not fair to use the license dollar of upland hunters, big-game hunters, and black-bass fishermen to pay for a glut of hatchery trout. There are just so many slices of pie in a sportsmen's fund.

Wherever possible, and in some states it will be impossible in the foreseeable future, there is sure to be increasing emphasis on the only intelligent solution, a clean-up of waters that will permit healthy natural reproduction together with a sizable carry-over of fish released. This is a major goal of every national angling association and it is no impossible dream. Although some hold the concept utopian, members of the Atlantic Salmon Association have already succeeded in a partial cleansing of northeastern rivers, such as the Connecticut and the Merrimack. Trout Unlimited and the Isaak Walton League have led an inland crusade, and there are local groups that have won battles.

Ensuring the future of trout and salmon through restoration of the environment can be a thankless task, since results are rarely immediately apparent. A lot of otherwise intelligent folk vote for fish now, not sometime in the future. Nobody questions the wisdom of restoration, yet there is counter-battery when dedicated biologists attempt to bring back a stream. The vicious circle is there.

A given state agency is mandated to provide so many pounds of fish-flesh per year, actually an outdated concept based on quantity rather than quality. Trained culturists may peer over their spectacles, aware that sociological put-and-take offers no long-range dividends and is outrageously expensive—but demand is there and administrators aim to please. So we get hatchery strains that grow rapidly and find it difficult to cope with life after release. Too often they are dumped into mudholes hardly capable of all-year bluegill and horned pout survival.

Today a hatchery trout can be produced that is vividly colored. It's all a matter of food content in the rearing pools,

A rainbow is brought to hand on Tennessee's Tellico River. (Photo by Erwin A. Bauer)

perhaps a dash of paprika and alfalfa larded into prepared pellets. The flesh of the fish is pink, but doesn't taste like a wild trout. No matter, cosmetics help to keep citizens satisfied. Fisheries technicians rarely go fishing; they know too much about the generally inferior product turned loose.

This will change in the foreseeable future, if only because the public is becoming educated. Quantity must yield to quality wherever there are suitable waters, although put-and-take with its attendant fast-growing and short-living strains is sure to die hard. Fish culturists know how to rear the better breeds, but there are roadblocks. Most of these premier grades mature slowly and react adversely to rough handling. They are high strung thoroughbreds; however, once released in a favorable environment they have a survival capability far beyond that of the tame and pampered quick-turnover fishes. Aquatic biologists have the tools and the knowledge; they need only a ground-swell of encouragement from citizens united.

Those aforementioned exotics will be treated very gingerly in the future, since their introduction has proved a tricky business at best. There is always danger in tampering with a natural balance, even though a species to be introduced is native to an area of release. Landlocked salmon seem to find competition with brown trout difficult, and there is the historic decline of aureolus (the eastern golden trout) in Lake Sunapee, New Hampshire, after lakers were brought in. Hybrids, such as the splake and tiger, do not reproduce, so there is a measure of control.

Somebody will immediately remind me of the success of coho and chinook salmon in the Great Lakes. That is a latter-day phenomenon made possible by a tremendous supply of forage, yet it could backlash in the future if baitfishes are decimated or suffer an epizootic.

Coho have not fared so well on the North Atlantic seaboard where they have been stocked, admittedly in minimal numbers but with much fanfare, by the states of Massachusetts and New Hampshire. It is my feeling that salmon smolts there are harried by successive waves of summer bluefish. In any event, the fishery has yet to move beyond a target of opportunity stage. Angler-success ratios remain low, although there is meager success in natal rivers during fall spawning runs. Pacific salmon have been stocked, always futilely to date, in a number of New England fresh water lakes.

237

Recent years have seen much pressure to introduce land-locked striped bass, and proponents point to the success of a striper population in South Carolina's Santee-Cooper impoundment. They forget that the sea-going bass must have a vast amount of forage to survive. Santee-Cooper fills this requirement with a bloom of gizzard shad, yet a striped bass will eat anything that does not eat him first. Therefore, released in a lake that lacks abundant foodstuffs, bass will feast on whatever is available and, having cleaned out the kitchen, must expire. If there happens to be a resident population of trout, they will serve as snacks for the voracious bass. Any exotic may be spectacular for a while. Then we pay the bill.

It is the nature of man to experiment, and this is laudable. Unfortunately, human beings can be quite as stubborn as they are talented, so we witness a dogged determination to reinforce failure. If a project doesn't work, that ought to be the end of it until such time as controlled research offers a new approach. However, if funds can be appropriated, you can be sure that an experiment will muddle along—impossible, lost and barren, wasting license dollars. It becomes make-work instead of progress and the charlatans will fight like tigers defending their cubs to continue tilting at windmills.

There will be less of this as citizens demand first things first: abatement of pollution, a cleaning of river systems, adequate fishways over barrier dams, and strict enforcement of laws prohibiting the planned destruction of a living ecosystem. Trout fishermen will always be a minority, so we must convince the multitudes that clean waters are essential to all life.

When history gets around to leveling about this period, there may well be reference to a delaying action that hurt, but failed. During the mid-60s and early 70s, America suffered a wave of eco-freaks. Many were well meaning, fueled by emotion and unfortunately bereft of any knowledge about fish or wildlife. They espoused a rather senseless crusade dedicated to an absolute retreat from the scientific management of natural

Anglers prospect the Rio Grande running through a box canyon in northern New Mexico. (Photo by Russell Tinsley)

resources. Not a grass stem was to be cut, no mature or tottering tree could be felled, no fish or game harvested.

It seemed idealistic and a percentage of Americans bought it for a short time. Then, of course, thinking citizens realized that the most radical of these agitators had no grasp of intermeshing nature, but were simply chanting parrot lines invented by leading extremists. Typical was an emotional statement

239

made at a joint meeting of lumbermen and environmentalists in New England to discuss use of a short-lived pesticide to control spruce budworm, then threatening to wipe out northern conifers.

A furious young man declared, to the wild applause of a few fellow-travelers, "I think it would be better to let all trees die than to kill a single bald eagle!"

Harm lay in the fact that people of intelligence, although not highly educated in the field of natural resource management, listened to such strident, far-out clamor and reached the conclusion that *all* conservationists are rabid fruitcakes! Even a schoolchild can understand that if trees and game fish are destroyed, then birds are doomed as well.

Fortunately, that's a thing of the past. Today's strong environmental crusaders are using their minds and they are far from negative. The ridiculous nonsense of the hot-eyed zealots has been consigned to sorry memory. There is a return to sanity and a healthy interchange of views between lay environmentalists and professionals in the field.

Trout? The storehouses are not inexhaustible, but we will preserve a heritage. Soon we are going to realize that coordination of effort is necessary to preserve a birthright threatened by holier-than-thou on the right and do-nothing on the left. This will come about. A few million sportsmen, aided by many millions who never seek fish or game, but who insist upon immediate upgrading of the environment, must prevail.

Tomorrow will see more air-clear rivers and birdsong—and black flies! There will be Walton's (and Arnold Gingrich's) cowslips and silver streams. Barring nuclear warfare or a return to abject mismanagement of natural resources, the children of Year 2000 are bequeathed that deep-breathing thrill occasioned by a trout rising as unfettered and wild and free as it might have been on the morning of creation.

Index

Index